FOUR TOOK FREEDOM

The aim of Zenith books is to present the history of minority groups in the United States and their participation in the growth and development of the country. Through histories and biographies written by leading historians in collaboration with established writers for young people, Zenith Books will increase the awareness of minority group members of their own heritage and at the same time develop among all people an understanding and appreciation of that heritage.

Dr. JOHN HOPE FRANKLIN, Chairman of the History Department at the University of Chicago, has also taught at Brooklyn College, Fisk University, and Howard University. For the year 1962–63, he was William Pitt Professor of American History and Institutions at Cambridge University in England. He is the author of many books, including *From Slavery to Freedom, The Militant South, Reconstruction After the Civil War,* and *The Emancipation Proclamation.*

SHELLEY UMANS is Director of the Center for Innovation for the Board of Education of the City of New York, a specialist in reading instruction, and a member of the instructional staff of Teachers College, Columbia University. For more than ten years, she has been a consultant to many major urban school systems throughout the United States. She is the author of *New Trends in Reading Instruction, Designs For Reading Programs,* and co-author of *Teaching the Disadvantaged.*

PHILIP STERLING was formerly associated with CBS Radio where he was Assistant Director of Press Information. He is the author of *Laughing on the Outside,* and co-author of *Polio Pioneers* and *Fiorello La Guardia.*

DR. RAYFORD W. LOGAN is a professor of history at Howard University in Washington, D.C. He has written numerous books, including *The Negro in American Life and Thought—The Nadir: 1877–1901* and *The Negro in the United States: A Brief History.* Dr. Logan is also the author of many articles for magazines and journals, and has traveled and lectured in many parts of the world.

CHARLES WHITE has studied at the Art Institute of Chicago, the Art Students League of New York and at Taller de Grafica in Mexico. He is the recipient of many awards, including a gold medal from the International Graphic Show in 1960.

Other Outstanding Zenith Books

A GLORIOUS AGE IN AFRICA, by Daniel Chu and Elliot Skinner. The story of three great African empires.

GREAT RULERS OF THE AFRICAN PAST, by Lavinia Dobler and William A. Brown, with special consultant Philip Curtin. Five African rulers who led their nations in times of crisis.

A GUIDE TO AFRICAN HISTORY, by Basil Davidson, revised and edited by Haskel Frankel. A general survey of the African past from earliest times to the present.

LIFT EVERY VOICE, by Dorothy Sterling and Benjamin Quarles. The lives of Booker T. Washington, W. E. B. Du Bois, Mary Church Terrell, and James Weldon Johnson.

PASSAGE TO THE GOLDEN GATE, by Daniel Chu and Samuel C. Chu. A history of the Chinese in America to 1910.

PIONEERS AND PATRIOTS, by Lavinia Dobler and Edgar A. Toppin. The lives of six Negroes of the Revolutionary era. '

TIME OF TRIAL, TIME OF HOPE, by Milton Meltzer and August Meier. The Negro in America, 1919–1941.

THE UNFINISHED MARCH, by Carol Drisko and Edgar A. Toppin. The Negro in the United States, Reconstruction to World War I.

WORTH FIGHTING FOR, by Agnes McCarthy and Lawrence Reddick. A history of the Negro in the United States during the Civil War and Reconstruction.

FOUR TOOK FREEDOM

The Lives of Harriet Tubman, Frederick Douglass,
Robert Smalls, and Blanche K. Bruce

PHILIP STERLING and
RAYFORD LOGAN, Ph.D.

Illustrated by Charles White

ZENITH BOOKS
DOUBLEDAY & COMPANY, INC., GARDEN CITY, NEW YORK

The Zenith Books edition, published simultaneously in hardbound and paperback volumes, is the first publication of *Four Took Freedom*.

Zenith Books edition: 1967

Library of Congress Catalog Card Number 65–17229
Copyright © 1967 by Doubleday & Company, Inc.
All Rights Reserved
Printed in the United States of America
9   8   7   6   5   4

CONTENTS

HARRIET TUBMAN

CHAPTER I

MOSES WORE SKIRTS
⊱ Harriet Tubman ⊰

She was black and little. She was hungrier than any seven-year-old ought to be. No wonder. Since early morning she had sat on the floor holding Mistress Sarah's baby in her lap, crooning, whispering, scolding, jiggling. If the baby cried, she was whipped.

When breakfast time came, she limbered her puny muscles while baby was fed by mother. Now, standing close to the table in the sunny dining room of the Big House, Harriet was waiting to "take over" again. Miss Sarah, engaged in a shouting, name-calling quarrel with her husband, didn't see her.

The noise and anger meant nothing to the girl. She had ears only for the rumblings in her empty little belly and eyes only for the lumps of sugar lying in a silver bowl. Slowly her hand moved across the white table-cloth. If she made it, she would know for the first time what real sugar tasted like. It didn't happen. Miss Sarah turned around—and saw!

"Don't you dare, you little black wretch!" The mistress reached for a rawhide strap. Harriet ran. Out the back door, past houses and kennels, stockpens and corn

cribs . . . "Show me a hiding place, Lord. Show me a
hiding place . . ." Exhausted, she leaned against the
side of a pigpen and looked into it. "This'll have to do,
Lord. Thank you." She hid there from Friday till Tues-
day. Then she crept back and took her whipping.

Harriet was born in 1820 or 1821* on the farm of her
master Edward Brodas near Bucktown, in Dorchester
County, Maryland. Before she was six, she was hired
out. Her first mistress whipped her almost daily. Another employer kept her working outdoors though she
was ill with measles. Then he dumped her, half-dead,
at the Brodas place, growling "She ain't worth the meal
and molasses to keep her alive. Give her back to her
mammy."

Little Hatt became well enough to be hired out again.
Time after time she was brought back, her body torn by
whippings, her soul hurting with helpless anger. Her
mother, Rit (for Harriet), would spread lard on her
wounds, feed her and lecture her.

"You don't *have* to be so uppitty with white folks, *do*
you?"

"Don' know 'bout that," Hatt would mumble.

Her brothers, Benjamin, William, Henry, James, Robert, and John, had comforting words and smiles for her.
So did her sister, Mary Ann.

Worthless and troublesome as a house servant, Harriet was put to work outdoors. Planting, hoeing, guiding
a plow, splitting wood slowly strengthened her. Grow-

* Records of slave families were not carefully kept.

Worthless and troublesome as a house servant, Harriet was put to work outdoors.

ing, she did not outgrow her hatred of slavery. It burned slow and hot. When it flared into words, her father, Ben Ross, might say, "I know, Hatt, I know. But ain't nothin' you can do just yet, except please your master and put your trust in God."

Was that all? Not quite. In August 1831, Nat Turner, a slave and a preacher, stormed through southern Virginia with seventy others, killing masters and freeing slaves. It took three U. S. Army regiments to stop them. For fear and revenge, white Virginians killed at least 120 Negroes. Turner himself was not caught until October 30. News of what was happening whispered its way to the Brodas slave cabins with amazing speed. All day long young Hatt's hand was at her task but her mind was on Turner. The sickle she swung was not just mowing wheat. It was cutting down his enemies.

Hanging Turner that November didn't make the slaveholders feel safer. More night patrols were put on the roads. More bloodhounds were bought. The overseer's voice grew harsher, his whip cracked harder. But if these added pressures forced slaves to think less about using guns, news from the North made them think more about using their feet.

Facts and ideas could not be kept from them. There were always some who could read. The rest had eyes, ears and wit which they used to learn about the big happenings in the outside world. So Harriet knew there were people in the North, mostly whites but some Negroes, talking, writing, holding demonstrations for the abolition of slavery. She heard about the Underground

Railroad, a secret network of Abolitionists who helped runaways get to freedom. It wasn't a real railroad with tracks and steam engines, of course. But the people who worked in it fell into the habit of using railroad language, so that outsiders would not understand them. They called themselves "agents," "conductors," "forwarders." They spoke of their homes and other hiding places as "stations" and the runaways were "passengers."

Many Abolitionists were Quakers. They were non-violent Christians who believed that no man had a right to enslave another. Some of them died for that belief. In nearby Bucktown, there was at least one Quaker lady.

"Some day," young Hatt promised herself, "I'm goin' to knock on that lady's door."

At fifteen Harriet was hired as a field hand to a farmer named Barrett. Only five feet tall, she was broad-shouldered, well-muscled, and on her way to being stronger than most men. In the fall, there was evening work to do. One evening, Harriet noticed Jim, a Barrett slave, take the road toward the village store. The overseer followed. If Jim could get back to work before the overseer found him, he'd save himself a whipping. Harriet cut through the fields to warn him. At the store she found both men. Advancing toward Jim, the overseer called:

"You, Hatt. Get me that rope off the nail and help me tie this black scoundrel."

Hatt stood motionless. Jim, circling toward the door,

Harriet was hired as a field hand to a farmer named Barrett.

suddenly darted into the night. Hatt sprang to the doorway and blocked it with her short powerful body. Beside himself with rage, the overseer snatched a two-pound weight from the counter and hurled it at the running man. It hit Harriet a crushing blow on the forehead. She sank to the floor.

She lived though no one thought she would. The lump of iron left a deep, scarred dent. For the rest of her life she would have sudden sleeping spells, as though a pressure on her brain were cutting off the current that made her go.

By spring her hand was on the plow again. Most people thought her witless now. She let them think what they pleased. She was thinking about something else . . .

"Freedom, freedom. How do you get free, Lord?"

When her owner, Edward Brodas, died, her new master, a Dr. Thompson, allowed her to hire out if she supported herself and brought him a dollar a week. If she had anything left over, it was hers to keep.

"Hatt, you got a chance now," her father said. "You can save some money and maybe buy yourself free." But at the rate she was going, it would take a lifetime.

At twenty-four, Harriet met John Tubman, a young freeman. She loved him and married him, only to find out after five years that she loved freedom more. To John, Hatt's freedom didn't matter as long as he had his own and she was around to look after him.

From early childhood Harriet lived in fear of a greater agony than whipping—the auction block. Brodas had tried to sell her soon after she recovered from her head injury. She saved herself by acting dull-witted; he sold others instead.

For several years after Brodas' death, and with John Tubman sharing her cabin, the thought of being sold seldom crossed Hatt's mind. But in 1849, the plantation was upset by a death in the master's family, and fear swept through the slave quarters again. Hatt sought out two of her brothers.

"Trader struttin' 'round Bucktown," she said. "Comin' here tomorrow."

"Why you tellin' us?" one of them asked.

"I'm gonna be gone. Both of you come with me."

"What about John?" the other brother asked.

"John'll keep," she said. "Freeman don't have to slip away. He can come when I send for him, if he likes."

The brothers wouldn't risk it, so Harriet made plans of her own. Under her shapeless dress she tied a slim cotton sack holding a sharp bowie knife and what little food and money she had in the world. Next she lingered near the back door of the Big House where she was sure her sister, Mary Ann, could hear her singing. Mary Ann would get the message:

Steal away, steal away, steal away to Jesus!
Steal away, steal away home,
I ain't got long to stay here.

My Lord, He calls me,
He calls me by the thunder,
The trumpet sounds it in my soul,
I ain't got long to stay here.

Then she made her move—into the woods and away from slavery.

She was an outlaw now. When they found her gone, the man-hunting dogs would get some exercise. There would be patrols along the roads, guards at the bridges and posters on the walls offering a big-money reward for her capture. No matter. She knew what she needed to know. Moss growing thick and green on tree trunks would point her north by day. The North Star's faint, steady pinpoint of light would guide her through the darkness.

Keeping the star in front and to the left, she made her way along the wooded bank of the Choptank River. When the silence and blackness of the hours before dawn stroked her spirit with icy fingers, she sang the old freedom song:

When Israel was in Egypt land, let my people go.
Oppressed so hard they could not stand,
Let my people go.
Go down, Moses, way down in Egypt land,
Tell Ol' Pharaoh, to let my people go.

Where the Choptank ended, she kept on northeast to Ezekiel Hunn's farm, an Underground Railroad station at Camden, Delaware.

"Miss Parsons, the Quaker lady in Bucktown, told me you could help me," said Hatt.

Hunn brought her to his brother, John, in Middletown. From there she went to New Castle, then to Wilmington, where Thomas Garrett, a Quaker shoe merchant, sheltered runaways in the rooms above his store. Then, one more wagon ride due north, a short walk to the Pennsylvania line and—she was free! Years later, she told a friend how it felt:

"I looked at my hands to see if I was the same person. There was such a glory over everything. The sun came like gold through the trees and over the field and I felt like I was in Heaven."

Except for one thing. She would have to be on guard against slave catchers. They were allowed by law to hunt down runaways in the free states and bring them back to their masters. It was a profitable business for cruel, cutthroat types who were too smart to be outright criminals. But less than twenty miles away, in the midst of Philadelphia's large Negro population, she could find help, advice, and safety. She arrived there by sundown.

For more than a year Harriet worked as laundress, scrubwoman, cook, seamstress, changing jobs often, just to enjoy her newfound liberty.

All the while she yearned for her family. She was made for freedom but not for loneliness. Hoping to get news from home, she visited William Still at the office of the Philadelphia Vigilance Committee. As Corresponding Secretary, Still, a free Negro, kept in touch with Underground Railroad agents in the slave states. There was no news and she decided there was only one way to get it.

"Mr. Still," she said one day, "could you please carry a letter to John Bowley down Cambridge way? He's my sister's husband and he's free. But Mary Ann and the two children ain't."

"I'll do my best," Still replied. "What shall I write?"

"Tell him to hire a fishing boat in Cambridge and sell fish around town till they get used to his hiring a boat. He gets the three of them aboard one day and he can sail straight up Chesapeake Bay to Bodkin's Point. I'll be there to bring them to Baltimore and on through."

"Baltimore is a dangerous place, Harriet. Full of slave catchers and idle ruffians."

Harriet's face hardened. "I'll take my chances. They're my folks and I'll bring 'em out myself." Still wrote the letter.

John Bowley was ready in December 1850. None too soon. Mary Ann's master suddenly decided to sell her. Bowley had to "steal" his wife from the slave pen in the courthouse while the auctioneer and the bidders were at lunch. Somehow all four reached their boat and sailed safely to the appointed place. Harriet was waiting. With the help of Still's agents, she brought them north, rejoicing. She had struck a blow, unafraid, against the power of the slaveholders. Victory was sweet and strong in her mind, like the wine she had once tasted in a Philadelphia lady's kitchen. She would work in anybody's kitchen till she "fell out" to get enough money together for another trip south. "Yes . . . tell ol' Pharaoh to let my people go!"

A few months later Harriet went south again. She brought back three men, including her brother, John

Ross. Then, in the fall of 1851, she went down to Dorchester County to find John Tubman. She needn't have bothered. She learned John was married again. The bitterness of her disappointment did not send her north alone. Ten slaves-no-more came to Philadelphia with her.

Soon after, Hatt made a fourth trip, through new December snow. From a cheerless hideout in the woods she sent word to her brother, James. Many times, later that day, he sang for chosen listeners:

> *When that old chariot come,*
> *I'm going to leave you . . .*

Some of them, without looking up from their work, sang a soft reply:

> *When that old chariot comes,*
> *I'm a-goin' with you . . .*

James, his wife, and nine others met Harriet that night and started out. She knew the way well by now, but the journey was longer, more dangerous. The new Fugitive Slave Act of 1850, harsher than earlier laws, made the North more unsafe for runaways. The Underground Railroad therefore stretched its line into Canada. Harriet took her group across the Niagara Falls International Bridge to St. Catharines, some 500 miles northwest of Philadelphia. From that time, for more than six years, she considered St. Catharines her home, though she was seldom there.

Harriet went south time after time and always came back with "a trainload of passengers." The gun-slinging,

Harriet led over 300 slaves to freedom and never lost a passenger.

whip-swinging night patrollers didn't bother her. Neither did the man-hunting dogs or the posters saying she was "wanted." She trusted in the Lord, all right, but she wasn't letting it go at that. Leading slaves from bondage was her job now, and she kept on learning how to do it better.

For those who wanted to turn back, she had a pistol and a word of advice: "Live North or die here."

For babies whose coughing or crying might betray their hiding place, she carried sleeping medicine. For those who fell ill, she brewed comforting drinks from roots and herbs. Sometimes her own strange sleeping spells overtook her for a few minutes or an hour. When she woke, she would count heads and say, "Let's move on."

Shortly before Christmas, 1854, Jacob Jackson, a free Negro in Dorchester County, received a letter from his adopted son, William Henry, in the North:

"Read my letter to the old folks and give them my love, and tell my brothers to be always watching unto prayer and when the good old ship of Zion comes along, to be ready to step aboard."

William Henry didn't have any old folks or brothers. But Harriet did. Old Jacob lost no time telling Benjamin, Henry, and Robert that their sister Hatt was on her way. When Benjamin met her in secret the day before Christmas, he said, "No time to lose, Hatt. Miss 'Liza swear she's gonna put us on the block Monday."

"We'd best start tonight," said Harriet. "Tell John

Harriet went south time after time and came back with passengers of all ages.

Chase, Peter Jackson, and Janie Kane we'll meet right here. You bring Henry and Robert."

"Gonna be hard on Henry," Benjamin frowned. "His Harriett Ann's about to have a baby."

Hatt bowed her head. "We can't wait. Tell him we'll be in the fodder house next to our folks' cabin till late Christmas night. It's a long way but he could catch up." Henry did catch up, after lingering to see his newborn baby.

Old Rit was expecting these three sons for Christmas, but neither they, nor Harriet who had not seen her mother in five years, dared show themselves. She must not know they had passed that way. But they did send John Chase to bring Ben Ross to the door of the fodder house, and the old man talked to his fine sons and his quiet fierce daughter in the darkness without seeing or touching them. When they left, he said his goodbyes with a bandanna tied over his eyes. To the men who came to ask about his children, he could say, "I never laid eyes on them."

Reaching Philadelphia, Hatt and her brothers told their story to William Still. He wrote in his Vigilance Committee record:

"Harriet Tubman had been their Moses. She had faithfully gone down into Egypt and delivered these six bondsmen by her own heroism. Her like, it is probable, was never known before . . ."

Hatt often thought about bringing her aging parents to Canada. She held back for fear the trip would be too hard on them. When she heard, in 1857, that Old Ben was in trouble for helping another slave run off, she knew it was then or never.

In a secret midnight reunion with Ben and Rit, Harriet learned her father was to be tried in the Cambridge courthouse the following Monday.

"Don't you fret yourself none," said Harriet solemnly. "We are about to move papa's trial to a higher court." Then she went to work. She found the skeleton of an old two-wheel buggy—wheels, axle, and the long shafts between which the horse is hitched. Across the shafts she fastened a board large enough to carry the three of them. Someone, probably old Rit, plaited a straw harness collar. Somehow, Harriet got herself an old horse to pull her freedom chariot.

They started late at night. By morning they were far enough from home to make it safe for Ben and Rit to get on a train. She gave them forged passes and a story to tell if they were questioned. Then Hatt drove her shaky contraption to Wilmington, met her parents at Thomas Garrett's house and took them to St. Catharines.

Dr. Thompson's sullen, iron-muscled wench of bygone years had become a menace. In Maryland's Big Houses, slaveholders catalogued her "crimes." She came and went as she pleased, leading their "property" north by the dozen and the score. Worse, her example was encouraging hundreds of other slaves to flee. And she was feeding the discontent of all the rest. Periodically they offered new rewards for her dead-or-alive capture until the total over the years was $40,000.

But in the slave cabins they called her "Moses." She was becoming a hotly whispered legend, like Nat Turner before her:

"She go bent an' shufflin' through Cambridge, totin' a basket of truck. Ain't nobody gonna pay no mind to an old woman like that . . ." "Yeah, and all the time she got a pistol hid in there . . ." "When the catchers get on her track headin' north, she gets on a train goin' south . . ." "She slide into Bucktown by daylight one time, carrying two live chickens, lookin' like she had business to be around. Then here come ol' Massa Stewart down the street, knows her from way back. She let them chickens run loose and took after them, real awkward-like. Massa Stewart laughed so hard he never did get a look at her."

In the North she was welcomed with respect and admiration to the comradeship of abolitionism. Her circle of friends grew wider. In Peterboro, New York, her "passengers" hid on the huge estate of Gerrit Smith. Frederick Douglass, himself a famous runaway, found food and beds for them in Rochester. William H. Seward, the U. S. Senator who became President Lincoln's Secretary of State, provided a house and land for Hatt, Rit, and Ben when they moved to Auburn, New York, late in 1857.

All Harriet wanted was to keep at it. To raise money for more trips, she told the story of her work at conventions and public meetings. She was an honored guest in the Concord home of the philosopher, Ralph Waldo Emerson, and other Boston Abolitionists. Thomas Wentworth Higginson, Unitarian minister in Worcester, wrote to his mother:

"We have had the greatest heroine of the age here, Harriet Tubman, a black woman and a fugitive slave . . . She has had a reward of $12,000 offered for her in Maryland and will probably be burned alive whenever she is caught."

No one down there ever got up early enough or stayed up late enough to catch her. She kept on with it until

December 1860. In ten years she made nineteen trips to the South and brought back three hundred fugitive slaves, not counting hundreds of others who took courage from her example without ever having seen her.

In the North, anger against the Fugitive Slave Law was at the exploding point. Setting out for Boston to attend a conference, Harriet stopped a few days in Troy, New York to visit friends.

"Folks around town seemed kind of edgy as I passed through," she said to her host.

"No doubt," he replied. "Virginia slave-catchers are holding Charles Nalle in the jail. He's coming up before Commissioner Beach tomorrow for a hearing. There may be serious trouble."

There was a crowd in front of the Commissioner's office the next morning and Harriet was in its midst. As the crowd grew, Harriet walked, hunched and bent, to the guard at the entrance. She seemed so harmless they allowed her to go to the second-floor office where Nalle was held. Slowly she edged her way toward him. Suddenly Nalle broke from his guards, ran to the window, opened it and stepped out on the ledge. Before he could jump, the guards hauled him back inside. Surrounded by armed men, he was marched downstairs. Harriet dropped the basket she was carrying, sprang to the still open window and shouted:

"Here he comes! Take him!"

Then she plunged down the stairs, butted a guard out of the way and locked arms with the handcuffed prisoner. Unable to break her grip on Nalle, the guards dragged both of them along the street, clubbing Harriet to make her let go. Harriet hung on. Above the crowd's angry growl, Harriet's voice rose:

"Take him, friends! Drag him to the river! Drown him but don't let him go back to slavery!"

It was a battle cry. The crowd swarmed over the policemen and their pro-slavery supporters. Fists flew and clubs swung. Harriet and Nalle were knocked to the ground but she never loosened her hold on him. Nalle's chained wrists were bleeding, Harriet's clothes were torn, her shoes gone, her body bruised. The battle boiled its way slowly, bloodily, to the waterfront. Nalle stumbled into a waiting skiff and the boatman made for the opposite shore of the Hudson River.

"He's not safe yet," Harriet shouted. "The Commissioner will telegraph ahead." Four hundred men and women, fighting mad, charged aboard the steam ferry that was about to make its midday crossing. Nalle, captured at pistol point by a constable on the far shore, was being held in the barricaded office of a police court judge. The crowd stormed the building despite gunfire from the inside. The door was smashed open by a giant of a man who fell a moment later under a blow from a deputy sheriff's hatchet. In the midst of the fighting, Harriet and another woman carried the almost unconscious Nalle out, loaded him into a buggy going north. He arrived in Canada two days later, but he came back even before the Civil War began. Since the people of Troy had guts enough to save him, he wanted to make it his home.

Harriet Tubman had met all kinds of Abolitionists but never anyone like John Brown. There *wasn't* anyone like him. For three years Brown and his five sons fought in a small civil war in Kansas to decide whether it would be a slave territory or free, but the issue remained unsettled. Now he was convinced that the real freedom war had to be waged on the South's own soil. He had a plan. With shrewd leadership and good discipline, a small band of do-or-die fighters could grow stronger by raiding plantations and adding liberated slaves to their forces. Beginning in the states bordering the North, they would move southward until slavery was completely wiped out.

From Kansas, Brown came east to raise money, to recruit fighting men and one fighting woman, Harriet Tubman. In St. Catharines, Brown outlined his plan to help the slaves take their freedom, gun in hand.

"I'm with you," said Harriet. "What do you want me to do?"

For ten days, in April 1858, they talked about the Underground Railroad routes through Maryland, Delaware, and Pennsylvania which she knew so well. Brown made notes and marked his maps. When they parted Harriet promised to recruit men. Just before the blow was to be struck, she would join him. He was so impressed by her ability, courage and character that he called her, in all solemnity, "General Tubman." But since he could not bring himself to think of a general as "she," he wrote to his son:

"Harriet Tubman hooked on his whole team at once.

He is the most of a man, naturally, that I ever met with."

In the spring of 1859 Brown, under the name of Isaac Smith, rented a farm near Harpers Ferry, Virginia. Guns, ammunition, supplies were hidden in the barn. Now he needed Harriet and her recruits, but she was nowhere to be found. Traveling to enlist warriors in Brown's crusade, she had fallen ill. For weeks she lay in a New Bedford cottage, sunk in the sleeping spells she could not control, too weak to sit up and unable to think when she was awake. It was mid-September before Lewis Hayden, Negro Abolitionist leader in Boston, discovered her whereabouts and sent her a message: *"You must come to Boston at once."*

"To Boston? Why?"

Slowly she remembered . . . *John Brown!* She must be on her way to Boston, Albany, Troy, Auburn, St. Catharines to assemble her volunteers, if any were left after waiting so long for action. They must get to the Old Man, wherever he was. Too late! While Harriet struggled to force her mind and body back into fighting trim, John Brown and a band of twenty-one Negroes and whites captured the U. S. Arsenal at Harpers Ferry. Two days later it was all over. Ten of his men, including two of his sons, were dead. Brown was wounded and taken prisoner with six others by troops under the command of Colonel Robert E. Lee. All were found guilty of treason and sentenced to be hanged. Early on December 2, he wrote, *"I, John Brown, am quite certain that the crimes of this guilty land will never be purged away but with blood.*" Then he rode under guard through the sunlit, cloudless morning to the gallows.

Harriet Tubman's tears fell quietly. "It was not John Brown that died at Charlestown," she said. "It was Christ—the savior of our people."

Across the free states bells tolled, voices cried out in memory of John Brown. His deeds and his death gave new power to the anti-slavery movement. Northern political leaders knew they couldn't shrug their shoulders any longer. The South was shaken.

Both sides knew there was a showdown coming in the 1860 presidential election. Abraham Lincoln was not an Abolitionist but he was no pro-slavery man either. To the deep South he was a black Republican who talked too much about human rights. After he was elected, eleven states pulled out of the Union. All winter, in 1861, the divided halves of "this guilty land" waited to see which of them would fire the first shot. In April, Confederate shore batteries bombarded Fort Sumter, the United States Army installation in Charleston Harbor. And Harriet, trudging along a Boston street one spring morning, heard the young white men of an infantry regiment singing:

. . . John Brown died that the slave might be free,
But his soul goes marching on!

This was Harriet's war, too. She was going to get her licks in somehow. Carrying a letter from Massachusetts' Governor John Andrew, she reported to Brigadier General David Hunter at Hilton Head, one of the South

Carolina sea islands, in May 1862. Hunter, who knew her worth, briefed Harriet:

"As commander of the Union Army's Department of the South, I now hold the sea islands and the coast of South Carolina, Georgia, and Florida, but with less than 11,000 troops, mind you. From here we could fight our way up rivers far into enemy country. But I must also govern this territory because civilian government has broken down. When we came here, the whites ran *from* us and the slaves ran *to* us. More of them, men, women, children, come every day to Hilton Head, Port Royal, Beaufort. They are hungry, cold, sick, homeless but they won't go back to the plantations."

A smile flickered on Harriet's face. "That's natural. They're waiting to hear Mr. Lincoln say they're free."

"I'm waiting, too," Hunter replied. "I have the men for two black regiments here but Washington wants no Negro soldiers in this war. It fears to offend such border states as Maryland and Kentucky."

"General," said Harriet, "God won't let Mr. Lincoln beat the South till he does the right thing. He can do it by setting the Negroes free."

Hunter slapped the table top: "The day he calls them free men I will give them guns and send them after the rebels. Meanwhile, they are officially classed as *contrabands,* captured enemy property. I am assigning you to Surgeon Henry Durrant at the Contraband Hospital in Beaufort. While you work there, learn everything you can about the country and the people hereabouts. I have other tasks in mind for you."

First in Beaufort, South Carolina, and then up and down the coast, Harriet nursed contrabands and soldiers. She bathed fevered bodies, dressed wounds, delivered babies. Her gentle words were a kind of medicine, too.

"Most of the contrabands are very destitute, almost naked," she sent word to an old Abolitionist friend up North. "I am trying to find places for those able to work, and provide for them as best I can, while at the same time they learn to respect themselves by earning their own living." In Beaufort, with her own savings, she built a community washhouse so that contrabands could earn money doing Army laundry.

On January 1, 1863, President Lincoln issued the Emancipation Proclamation. By February there were two Negro regiments in the Union Army, one commanded by Colonel Thomas W. Higginson, Harriet's Abolitionist minister friend from Worcester, the other led by Colonel James Montgomery, a Kansas comrade-in-arms of John Brown.

Harriet's Underground Railroad talents were needed. She traveled through the rich plantation lands to set up a spy network among the Negro population. Her work helped Higginson and Montgomery make successful raids up the St. Marys River into Georgia, and up the St. Johns into Florida.

In June, she was with Colonel Montgomery aboard one of three gunboats carrying Negro troops up the Combahee River to raid the South Carolina back-country. Montgomery was in charge but it was Hatt's expedition. Mile by mile the boats chugged on, stopping when Harriet said, "Torpedo moored midstream, quarter of a mile from here" or "Rebs got a sentry post half a mile up." It was she and her agents who knew where to find and destroy Rebel supply dumps, where to ambush the Confederate troops that tried to fight back.

Returning, the boats brought 756 emancipated slaves to Beaufort. Without this labor supply, the Confederate troops in the area were in even deeper trouble.

After another year Harriet, weary, with a soldier's weariness, went back to Auburn. By the time she regained her strength the war was over. For a few months she worked as nurse and matron in the Contraband Hospital at Fortress Monroe, Virginia. On a train taking her back to Auburn, the conductor insultingly brushed aside the government pass which entitled her to half-fare. He ordered her to move to the baggage car. She refused. With the help of three white passengers, he dragged her, fighting, into the baggage car. She remained there all the way to New York, her arm and shoulder badly wrenched. The war had left her unhurt but peace inflicted a shameful wound.

There was something else, too. The U. S. Army owed her $1800 for her wartime services, but she could not collect it. Secretary of State Seward, General Hunter, Surgeon Durrant, prominent private citizens and two Congressmen tried to help her. They failed because the Federal books did not contain a rule that took care of black, free-lance heroines. Meanwhile she had her aging parents to support. Her second husband, Nelson Davis, a Civil War veteran whom she married in 1869, was ill with tuberculosis. And there were always three or four strangers whom she could not bear to turn away, eating and sleeping under her roof.

While Davis was well enough, he worked as a brickmaker. Harriet went from door to door in Auburn peddling chickens and vegetables she raised. Despite her poverty she found money to support two small schools for freedmen in the South.

The advancing years didn't turn her into a stay-at-home. She traveled to women's rights assemblies and was an ardent worker in the African Methodist Episcopal Zion Church. Harriet, turning sixty, then seventy, then eighty, kept working, speaking in public, asking little for herself and doing unto others. In 1890, after her husband died, she did get a government pension of eight dollars a month as a Civil War veteran's widow. By then she was seventy-nine years old. Eight years later the amount was increased to twenty dollars a month.

Since the time of her return from the war, Harriet had looked longingly at the 25-acre plot of land next to hers. She dreamed of establishing a home for whoever needed it, old, young, sick, well. It would be called the John Brown Home in memory of the man who died not alone for her people, but to end a nation's shame. Her chance came finally at an auction in 1896. Without a dime in her pocket she bid $1450 and got the property.

"Where are you going to get the money to pay for this land?" the amazed auctioneer asked.

"Don't you fret, son," Harriet answered. "Mr. Wood's bank will lend me the money right soon. This land's worth a sight more'n what I'm paying for it." The John Brown Home opened its doors to all comers in 1908, but closed them for good a few years after she died.

Nobody lives forever, not even the Harriet Tubmans of this world, but she made it into the new century, thirteen year's worth. Crippling rheumatism and sleeping spells forced her into a wheel chair but, awake, she still talked brightly of the past, hopefully of the future. And she could still sing "John Brown's Body" and "Go Down, Moses." If there were other Pharaohs in the land, she knew there would be another Moses, another John Brown. She died on March 10, 1913, at the age of ninety-three.

In June, the Mayor of Auburn proclaimed a city-wide day of tribute. The famous Booker T. Washington spoke and the Auburn Festival Chorus sang.

The old Tubman home on South Street is still maintained by the A. M. E. Zion Church and a bronze tablet is still fastened to the front wall of the country courthouse:

In Memory of Harriet Tubman . . . Called the "Moses" of her people . . . With rare courage, she led over three hundred Negroes up from slavery to freedom and rendered invaluable service as nurse and spy . . . She braved every danger and over-

*came every obstacle. Withal she possessed extraor-
dinary foresight and judgment so that she truth-
fully said—"On my Underground Railroad I never
ran my train off the track and I never lost a passenger."*

For Harriet Tubman death was not a defeat. She
marches with John Brown.

FREDERICK DOUGLASS

CHAPTER II

CUT OUT FOR A HERO
⊱ Frederick Douglass ⊰

Frederick Douglass wrote his own declaration of independence at the age of seventeen. He wrote it with his knuckles on the face of Edward Covey in a Maryland barn.

Covey was a "Negro breaker," a man who used his second-rate farm as a brutal "obedience training school" for slaves who displeased their masters. From January 1, 1834, till late summer he tried to destroy the spirit of manhood in young Fred by working him like an animal and whipping his back bloody with a wide cowhide strap. One mid-August Monday when Covey tried to whip him again, Fred grabbed the slave-breaker by the throat and flung him to the floor. Trembling with astonishment, Covey asked:

"Are you going to resist, you scoundrel?"

Politely, Fred replied, "Yes, sir."

The tall teen-youngster and the tough "man-tamer" fought for two hours. The farmer, combat-marked, called it quits by saying, "Now, you scoundrel, go to your work. I would not have whipped you half so hard if you had not resisted."

Douglass didn't feel whipped. Many years later he wrote:

"I was a changed man after that fight. I was nothing before—I was a man now. I had reached the point at which I was not afraid to die. When a slave cannot be flogged, he is more than half free."

The years that prepared him to stand against Covey were heavy years for a child to bear. He was born near Easton, Maryland, in February 1817 and was called Frederick Augustus Washington. His mother, Harriet, gave him her last name, Bailey. He saw her only a few times, after dark, when she walked twelve miles each way to visit him. She died when he was seven. His father was a white man whose name he could only guess.

Until Douglass was six he lived with his grandparents, Betsy and Isaac Bailey. Those were the happy years. Then he was sent to stay near his owner, Captain Aaron Anthony, in a yard full of other slave children ruled by Aunt Katy. She disliked, cuffed and starved him for three years. A coarse knee-length shirt was all he had to wear. At night he tried to keep warm by crawling head-first into a long sack on the damp packed-earth floor where he slept. He saw his beautiful Aunt Esther, bare-backed, bleeding, screaming for mercy under the furious bite of Captain Anthony's lash. He saw Nellie flogged in the presence of her five young children. And there were others, always others.

Just trying to stay alive, little Fred got some help from an unexpected source. Miss Lucretia, daughter of Captain Anthony, and wife of Captain Thomas Auld, was

Till he was six Frederick lived happily with his grandmother Betsy Bailey.

different than most Big House white ladies. She had some genuine pity in her heart. She washed away the blood and bandaged his forehead when another boy wounded him with a jagged cinder lump. And she gave him, a slave child, bread and butter!

Fred didn't just want to eat. He wanted to know things, too.

"Aunty, is all black people slaves?"

"No, child."

"Is all white people masters?"

"No, baby."

"How come we has to be slaves?"

"We born to it and we kept to it because *they* rules this land, same as Ol' Pharaoh ruled over Egypt. Yes . . ."

"Could I get free if I pray?"

"Depends how, honey. Some folks prays with their mouths, some prays with their hearts and souls, and some prays with their feet." What did *that* mean? He understood a few weeks later when his Aunt Jenny and Uncle Noah ran away, north to freedom.

When he was eight, Miss Lucretia said, "We're sending you to stay with Mr. Hugh Auld and Miss Sophia, my brother- and sister-in-law, and their son, Tommy. He's your age and you're going to be his boy for a while." Baltimore! Heaven! To Fred Bailey, standing there bug-eyed, one seemed as good as the other.

In the home of Hugh Auld, Fred ate, slept on a good straw bed, wore clean clothes and thrived on Miss Sophia's kindness. She saw nothing wrong in teaching

Fred to read when he asked her to. He learned quickly. Miss Sophia was so pleased that she told her husband.

Master Hugh put a stop to the lessons at once. The slave system insisted that Fred's mind had to be an empty locked room. Despite Hugh Auld, he had the key now. His mind was open and Fred invited the world to move in. He read everything in reach to find out everything he could—about everything.

Slowly Fred taught himself to write. In Hugh Auld's shipyard, he copied the writing which carpenters chalked on the timbers. He challenged other boys to writing contests on fences and sidewalks. They won, but he learned.

When Captain Anthony and Miss Lucretia died, Thomas Auld inherited Fred and brought him to his new plantation at St. Michaels. Starved and abused again, after seven years of good treatment in Baltimore, Fred could not hide his resentment. The last week of December 1833, Captain Thomas told him through clenched teeth, "New Year's Day I'm putting you out to Mr. Covey. *He'll* break you. By God, he will." That was the year Fred Bailey found out he wasn't afraid to die. After the fight in the barn, Covey never laid hands on him again.

The following year Fred was sent to work on William Freeland's plantation. He became close friends with Henry and John Harris, Sandy Jenkins, Charley Roberts and Henry Bailey. They would talk.

"Master Freeland don't skimp his hands on rations . . ." "He's never put a whipping on me . . ." "He's a good master . . ." "Why, you couldn't *buy* a better master!" Laughter. Then . . . "I want an even better one—*myself*." No laughter now. No more talk, but a silent mourning in each of them, for a long minute. And John Harris, in whispering tones, as though to himself:

> *O Canaan, sweet Canaan*
> *I am bound for the land of Canaan,*
> *I thought I heard them say*
> *There were lions in the way;*
> *I don't expect to stay much longer here.*

Another voice murmuring, "What you studying on, Fred?"

Fred told them: Master Hamilton's big canoe. All six of them. Start Saturday night. Paddle seventy miles up Chesapeake Bay. Then follow the North Star to a free state. He would write the passes.

When they were arrested the day before Easter, Fred managed to throw his forged pass into a fireplace. Henry Harris ate his on the way to the Easton jail. Sandy had betrayed them. The others were soon released but Fred spent a week expecting to be sold south—slow death instead of sudden freedom. Instead, Captain Thomas sent him back to Hugh Auld in Baltimore.

Hired out to Gardiner's shipyard, Fred took orders, insults and threats from the white workers, as well as a terrible beating from four who feared to face him singly. He also made friends in the Negro community, spoke in debates at the East Baltimore Mental Improvement

After attempting to escape, Frederick Douglass was put in jail.

Society and kept company with Anna Murray, a young free Negro woman. But he was sick of being *owned.* "Farewell, kind friends in Baltimore. Be patient, Anna Murray. I got freedom on my mind!"

Fred borrowed identification papers from a free Negro sailor who also supplied him with the kind of red shirt, waterproof hat, and black scarf that sailors wore. There could hardly be a greater, more dangerous act of friendship between a freeman and a slave.

Several times on his journey north, he saw or was seen by people who might have betrayed him but the closer Fred got to New York the less chance there was of meeting anyone he knew. He began to breathe easier, but when he did get there, it hit him. He didn't know a soul!

A seaman who saw Fred standing forlorn on a sidewalk brought him to David Ruggles, Negro secretary of the city's Underground Railroad committee. Ruggles hid him and sent for Anna Murray. She and Fred were married and immediately hurried farther north. In New Bedford, Massachusetts, they knocked on a door. It opened and they walked in. Nathan Johnson, expecting them, said, "Welcome." For a moment, that mid-September morning of 1838, the world stood still. Then they began a new life.

In order not to be discovered, Fred had called himself Johnson. New Bedford already had so many Johnsons of both colors that he picked another name, Douglass. And he was tired of being called Fred, too. From then on it was Frederick—Frederick Douglass. He found poor paying jobs while Anna took in washing. Between them they earned enough to set up a modest home of their own. Their daughter, Rosetta, was born in June 1839 and their son, Lewis, sixteen months later.

During their first New England winter, a young Abolitionist brought William Lloyd Garrison's paper, *The Liberator*, to the Douglass' door. Every new issue Douglass read turned on a storm in his mind.

"Anna, that man Garrison sets my soul on fire. This paper cries out the only real remedy for slavery—emancipation now!"

Frederick Douglass was hired out to a shipyard where he was brutally treated.

Douglass began to attend small Abolition meetings and to speak at them. In August 1841 he saw Garrison at last, and heard him, at an Anti-Slavery Society meeting in New Bedford. The next day he joined Garrison and forty other Abolitionists going to Nantucket for a three-day convention. There, William C. Coffin, a white New Bedforder, called on the twenty-four-year-old Douglass to speak. The tall light-skinned fugitive came forward. He trembled with stage fright but he told his five hundred white listeners about *being* a slave, and he told it like it was.

Douglass was immediately invited to be a traveling speaker for the Massachusetts Anti-Slavery Society at a salary of $450 a year. He wasn't sure he would do well at it. And appearing in public might just be asking Captain Auld to come and get him. But he agreed to try it for three months.

Almost from the beginning, Douglass was a great success. The newspapers rang with praise:

"This is an extraordinary man. He was cut out for a hero. As a speaker he has few equals. We have never seen a man with more real dignity . . ." "He has made color not only honorable but enviable . . ."

Even his white Abolitionist teammates were amazed. And at first, when he was just telling his experiences as a slave, they were very pleased. But he had ideas of his own. Alongside slavery, which remained his number one target, he would often line up another one—prejudice against Negroes in the free states. Then he would hit both in the same speech. He would talk about the separate church pews, the Jim Crow railroad cars and the job discrimination in the free states.

"You degrade us," he would say, "and then ask why we are degraded. You shut our mouths, and then ask why we don't speak. You close your colleges and seminaries against us, and then ask why we don't know more."

Though the Abolition leaders agreed with what he said, they began to worry about what the newspapers were printing:

"Douglass talks as well as men who have spent all their lives over books . . ." "He is pure in language, brilliant in thought . . ."

Finally they said, "Frederick, people won't believe you ever were a slave, if you keep on this way. Better have a little plantation speech than not. It is not best that you seem too learned."

Sure enough, some of his listeners did begin to have doubts. He didn't look, talk, or act like a slave. It came to him that after years of trying to cover up, he would have to *prove* who he used to be, though it might cost him his liberty. He wrote his story, putting in all the names, dates, and places he had kept out of his speeches. His *Narrative of the Life of Frederick Douglass, an American Slave* was published in May 1845. Almost overnight, it became a best-seller and Frederick Douglass became the most "wanted" runaway slave in the United States.

For safety's sake, he went to England where he did important work among the British friends of the Abolition movement. There were two more little Douglasses now, Frederick, Junior and Charles Remond, but the earnings of his book helped to support Anna and the children during his two-year absence. The famous runaway lectured in nearly all the big cities and towns of Ireland, Scotland, Wales, England. He met scholars, writers, clergymen, Members of Parliament, some of whom became his devoted friends. In a letter to Garrison he wrote:

"I live a new life. I breathe, and lo! The chattel becomes a man. I gaze around in vain for one who will question my equal humanity, claim me as a slave or offer me an insult. I am met by no upturned nose and scornful lip, to tell me—'We don't allow niggers in here.'"

Nevertheless, Douglass wanted to go home and his British friends raised $710.96 to buy Douglass his freedom from Thomas and Hugh Auld.

Home again, Douglass decided to publish a new antislavery newspaper in which Negroes could speak for themselves, on all subjects. To his surprise, Garrison and Wendell Phillips, another Abolitionist leader, raised objections.

"You have no experience as an editor," they said. "It will keep you from your work as a public speaker, and it will ruin you financially."

Moving to Rochester, New York, he set up a printing plant, the first to be owned by a Negro in the United States. For capital he used part of the $2100 his English friends had given him as a gift. The first issue, December 3, 1847, explained why Douglass had decided to publish the *North Star:*

"The man STRUCK is the man to CRY OUT. We must be our own representatives—not distinct from, but in connection with our white friends."

The *North Star** was a good paper, one of the best-edited of its time. The slaves' right to freedom and the free Negroes' right to full equality held first place in its columns but it had opinions and arguments to offer on many other subjects. Douglass was against flogging in the Navy, against capital punishment anywhere and against the Mexican War of 1846–48, from which the South hoped to gain new cotton lands.

The paper favored reforms to make it easier for poor people to get free government land. "What justice is there," the editor asked, "in the Government giving away millions and millions of acres of public lands, to aid the soulless railroad corporations to get rich? Multiply the free homes of the people . . ."

Negroes were not the only group being held down by law and public opinion. Women, too, were denied equal rights and opportunities. Understanding how close these two causes were to each other, Douglass played an important part in the first women's rights convention in 1848 and became a life-long advocate of full equality for women.

As a follower of Garrison, Douglass had believed free states should break away from the Union. The Garrison-

---

* The name was changed to *Frederick Douglass' Paper* in June 1851.

ians refused to vote in elections because they thought the U. S. Constitution compelled the Federal government to uphold slavery. True or not, the actions of Congress, the courts and every President up to Lincoln certainly made it look that way. The Garrisonians, therefore, fought against slavery only through the Underground Railroad and by public protest in their newspapers and mass meetings.

As an independent editor, Douglass began to agree with his friend Gerrit Smith that protest without political action was not enough. Congress had the power to pass laws against slavery, if the voters would use *their* power to elect anti-slavery Congressmen. In 1848, Douglass and other Negro Abolitionists attended the first convention of the Free Soil Party, which most free Negroes favored. This group nominated five anti-slavery candidates who were elected that year in addition to the ten already in Congress as Whigs or Democrats.

Garrison and his followers resented this change of mind but Douglass saw no conflict between protest and politics. While Garrison and Wendell Phillips were giving the Abolition movement heart, the anti-slavery Congressmen were giving it muscle.

Late that same year Douglass met a man who believed in still another kind of power. John Brown dreamed of setting up a string of small forts in the Allegheny Mountains and making armed freedom raids on the plantations. Some of the liberated slaves would go north by Underground Railroad. Others would ask for guns. As Brown's army grew, it would push deeper south.

Douglass, still a Garrison man, suggested that the slaveholders could be converted.

"Never," cried Brown. "They will never give up their slaves until they feel a big stick about their heads. I tell you, sir, the slaves themselves will have to take up arms. No people can have self-respect or be respected, who would not fight for their freedom!"

The young editor was disturbed but greatly impressed. He wrote of Brown as a white man who was— "in sympathy as deeply interested in our cause as though his own soul had been pierced by the iron of slavery."

Running the *North Star* was not a nine-to-five job for salary or profit. It was just one important task in the day and the lifetime of a man "standing on the watch tower of human freedom." Evenings, Douglass lectured in nearby cities. Mornings, he would find fugitives sitting on the stairway to his office. Editorial work would have to wait while he hid them and fed them. Once he had eleven runaways under his roof—eleven mouths to feed, eleven train tickets for Canada to buy.

Under the Fugitive Slave Act of 1850 any Negro could be claimed as another man's "missing property" in a hearing before a special U. S. Commissioner. There was no lawyer and no jury. The captive's fate was entirely up to the Commissioner, who was paid only five dollars for every Negro he turned loose but received ten for every one he sent south. Five dollars was a lot of money in those days but ten dollars was twice as much.

To help a runaway or protect him against Southern agents was worth a $1000 fine and six months in prison but Douglass went right on. In ten years he helped about four hundred fugitives on their way to Canada. His editorials and speeches raged against the Fugitive Slave Act in language that did John Brown's heart good. Speaking at the National Free Soil Convention of 1852, the ex-slave said:

"This infamous law is too bad to be repealed. It is fit only to be trampled under foot. The only way to make the Fugitive Slave Law a dead letter is to make half a dozen or more dead kidnapers."

Frederick Douglass' Paper stayed in business for thirteen years, until July 1860.* During most of that time, the big question was not only how to end slavery but how to keep it from spreading. North and South had tried to get along by a series of compromises worked out in Congress. When Missouri came into the Union as a slave state, Maine came in free. Slaveholding Texas was balanced by free Oregon. The Fugitive Slave Law was the price of California's admission as a free state.

Then Congress tried it one more time. In 1854 it passed the Kansas-Nebraska Bill, which allowed each of these two territories to decide for itself whether it wanted to be slave or free. Before there could be a fair election, the contest exploded into civil war, a small but savage curtain-raiser for the big one to come.

* From 1858 to 1863 there was also *Douglass' Monthly,* mainly for British readers.

For three years, Captain John Brown and five of his seven sons fought in Kansas to make it a free territory. But even out West, Brown never gave up his old dream. In February 1858 he lived three weeks in Douglass' house working out his plan to lead his guerrilla group into action. Shields Green, a South Carolina runaway staying with the Douglasses, became one of his best and bravest men. That August, Brown sent Douglass a message from Chambersburg, Pennsylvania: *Come; bring Shields Green; and as much money as possible.* They met secretly in a stone quarry guarded by Brown's followers.

"I am ready," said Brown.

"Where and how do you propose to begin?"

Brown explained. He would capture the U. S. Arsenal at Harpers Ferry, Virginia. He would load wagons with guns and ammunition. Then he would move twenty-five miles into the Blue Ridge Mountains to set up his first fortified camp.

"You will not free a single slave," said Douglass. "You are going into a perfect steel trap from which you will never get out alive."

They argued for two days but neither could change the other's mind. As they were about to part, Brown said, "Come with me, Douglass; I will defend you with my life." Douglass shook his head and turned to twenty-four-year-old Shields Green:

"I'm going home. If you want to come with me, you can." Green, sitting on a boulder, looked up and said quietly, "I b'lieve I'll go with the ol' man."

Near the end of his lecture in Philadelphia's National Hall Douglass saw friends off-stage signaling anxiously. Now, behind the scenes, one of them spoke in a low life-and-death voice:

"You must leave at once. John Brown and his men have been captured at Harpers Ferry. Governor Wise of Virginia has asked for your arrest."

"In that case, why am I still a free man?"

"A friend in the telegraph office. The Philadelphia sheriff won't receive the message until you are out of his reach."

Douglass didn't waste time. He knew his friendship with John Brown and Shields Green were enough to hang him in Virginia. He hurried to Rochester, to Canada, and then to England. There he read, heavyhearted, how the Old Man, Shields Green and five others had faced their executioners—proudly, without fear, without regret. Then a new grief, the death of his ten-year-old daughter, Annie, brought him home.

The mood of the country had changed. Abraham Lincoln was a candidate for President. Because he was against opening new territory to slavery, the slave states said they would leave the Union if he got himself elected. There was no room left for compromise.

When Confederate guns threw the Civil War's first shells at Fort Sumter, Frederick Douglass exclaimed, "God be praised." He understood it must turn into a fight to end slavery. But during the first year, Abraham Lincoln saw the Civil War differently. As a man, he

thought slavery was wrong. As President, he felt bound
to say:

"If I could save the Union without freeing *any* slave,
I would do it; and if I could save it by freeing *all* the
slaves I would do it; and if I could save it by freeing
some and leaving others alone, I would also do that."

There was no "if" about the war to Douglass, Garrison, Phillips, and the other Abolitionists in the newly
formed Emancipation League. The North was losing
support because it was still busy being kind to the slaveholders. It could win only by making Emancipation its
official policy.

"Make this an abolition war!" Douglass urged. He
considered the Union Army's refusal to take Negro recruits foolish and insulting.

"Why does the government reject the Negro?" he de-
manded. "Is he not a man? This is no time to fight
with your white hand and allow your black hand to be
tied!"

For eighteen months, Lincoln wrestled with deep
doubts. Then in September he decided to save the
Union by freeing some of the slaves and leaving others
alone. He issued a "preliminary proclamation" declar-
ing that all slaves would be free wherever there was still
a rebellion on January 1, 1863. Douglass lived in fear
that something might change the President's mind but
on New Year's night, Emancipation became a fact.

There was rejoicing in the South wherever the word
reached the enslaved. There were public celebrations in
the big cities of the North. In Boston's Tremont Temple

The Emancipation Proclamation of 1863 caused great excitement, celebration, and hope.

a capacity crowd waited from early evening until well past ten o'clock when a man rushed in shouting, "It's on the wires!" From his place on the platform Douglass could see the emotions of three thousand people turn on. The scene was wild and grand. He could hear the hallelujahs and the sobs. He could see the tears of thanksgiving. Nowhere did the news stir a greater storm than in the heart of Frederick Douglass—a storm of sadness for the past, triumph for the present, dreams for the future, and love for his people. It was Lincoln who had issued the proclamation but it was they who had overcome. This was no time for speeches. He sang, and the crowd sang with him:

> *Blow ye the trumpet blow . . .*
> *Let all the nations know . . .*
> *The year of Jubilee is come . . .*

Yes. But there was still a war to win. Negro army units began to form. Douglass recruited men for Massachusetts' two new colored regiments, the 54th and the 55th. His first volunteers were his sons, Lewis and Charles. Both fought, and Charles was wounded, at Fort Wagner where the 54th showed with 247 dead or wounded how gallant black men could be in the face of the deadliest fire. Other Negro troops gave the same proof in other battles. Before the Confederacy surrendered, 180,000 Negroes were in the Army and 29,000 in the Navy.

Meanwhile grievances developed. Negro soldiers were getting only half the pay of whites. They were not getting advancement for ability or bravery. Colored prisoners were being massacred by the Confederates. Douglass stopped recruiting and paid a call at the White House. Lincoln received him courteously. "I know who you are, Mr. Douglass," he said. "Sit down. I am glad to see you." He promised that in the end Negro soldiers would get equal pay. They did. The President also ordered that "for every soldier killed in violation of the laws of war, a rebel soldier shall be executed." From that first meeting, and from two others, Douglass went away deeply satisfied that he would never meet anyone more pure in heart. Lincoln had a high opinion of the man from Rochester, too. After her husband's death, Mrs. Lincoln sent the President's favorite walking stick to Douglass.

The war ended in April 1865. The 13th Amendment, prohibiting slavery in all the states forever, became law that December. Douglass began to hope he might be able to live his life quietly and privately but a long series of peacetime battles lay ahead.

The nation's newly liberated millions had no new way to live. They could only go back to work for their old masters. Andrew Johnson, made President by the bullet that killed Lincoln, had much more sympathy for the defeated slaveholders than for the freedmen.

Congress, however, was determined to keep the ex-Confederate states from running their affairs as though they had won the war instead of lost it. A Freedmen's Bureau, with local offices run by the Army, was set up to protect the interests of the former slaves in matters of health, education, personal welfare, labor contracts, and civil rights. A series of Reconstruction laws were passed in spite of Johnson. They included the 14th Amendment which said that no state shall "deprive any person of life, liberty or property without due process of law." Another law divided the South into five military districts under Army control.

In the election of 1868 the freedmen were able to vote for a President for the first time. As a Republican of national influence, Douglass contributed powerfully

Frederick Douglass visited Abraham Lincoln at the White House to ask for fair treatment for Negro soldiers.

to win the votes of 450,000 Negroes for Ulysses S. Grant. The general could not have become President without them. The Republican party now realized that Douglass was right to demand a law giving permanent Federal protection to the Negroes' voting rights. Thanks partly to his four years of public agitation, a 15th Amendment was added to the Constitution:

"The right of citizens of the United States to vote shall not be denied or abridged by the United States or any state on account of race, color, or previous condition of servitude."

Across the country a wave of celebrations followed. Ten thousand Baltimore Negroes paraded to Monument Square to hear Douglass speak.

"Educate your sons and daughters," he told them. "Show that besides the cartridge box, the ballot box and the jury box, you also have the knowledge box. We have a future; everything is possible for us."

The white ex-Confederates, however, yearned for the past. They began to set up a "new and improved" form of slavery which they called "keeping the Negro in his place." A secret special force, the Ku Klux Klan, was organized by Major General Nathan Bedford Forrest, a former slave-trader, whose troops had massacred almost three hundred captured Negro soldiers at Fort Pillow, Tennessee, in 1864. Trickery and sabotage were used to cripple the work of the Freedmen's Bureau. Negroes were threatened, whipped, or killed for building schoolhouses, voting, or refusing to work without knowing what their wages would be.

Nevertheless Negroes were sitting in the state legislatures and in Congress. They were proving themselves to be as able and as honest, and in some cases as dishonest, as their white colleagues. It seemed to Douglass that the freedmen's political strength would open all the doors to their future. As the nation's outstanding Negro spokesman, he believed it was his duty to be a leader in national politics.

Washington, a crossroads for the hundreds of important men, was where Douglass had to be. In 1870 he bought the *New Era,* a Washington Negro weekly founded earlier that year.

But Washington politics was a tricky game, even in those days. Douglass suddenly found himself forced to take sides in a strange dispute between his two most powerful friends, President Grant and Senator Charles Sumner, staunch defender of the freedmen's rights. The dictator of Santo Domingo offered the United States a chance to take over his Caribbean island country, peacefully, and Grant was for it. Sumner was against it. Douglass sided with Grant because United States rule would mean the abolition of slavery there.

When Grant made him a secretary to the special commission to visit the island, Douglass accepted, feeling no disloyalty to Sumner. His voyage aboard the USS *Tennessee* was amazingly different from his segregated boat trips before the war. Then he spent nights on the windswept decks huddling among the cotton bales. Now he took his meals at the captain's table. But—and there were more "buts" as the years went by—he got the old familiar taste of Jim Crow aboard another boat on the homeward voyage. Though he was traveling on the President's business, he was barred from the dining room. As for the Santo Domingo argument, the Senate backed Sumner and Grant had to give up his annexation plan.

Differing once again with Sumner, Douglass campaigned for Grant's re-election in 1872. Grant's opponent, Horace Greeley, was backed by a new group of "Liberal Republicans," including Sumner, and by the Democratic party. Both of these groups were sympathetic to the Northern businessmen who wanted to cool off the Reconstruction issue so they could invest their money in the South, profitably, peacefully. Horrified by this change of attitude on the part of many who had been "friends of the Negro," Douglass outdid himself on the speaker's platform.

"Tell me not of gratitude; talk to me not of deserting an old friend," he thundered. "No man is my friend who betrays the cause of my people. In front of us today we have the same old enemy, the same old snake in a new skin."

Greeley was badly beaten and Grant was swept back into office by a landslide. Douglass and Sumner, both men of high character, remained friends. It was Grant who slacked off his second term, but Sumner in the Senate kept fighting for the freedmen until his death in 1874. Douglass mourned for him, deeply.

That was a bad year. The whole country was suffering from a financial depression. The *New Era* failed and took $10,000 of Douglass' money with it. Many banks closed. Others hung on, fighting for their lives. Among these was the Freedmen's Savings and Trust

Company, started in 1865 to help freedmen build up some financial strength of their own. The trustees asked Douglass to become its president because they believed his reputation would keep the bank in business. But his reputation couldn't collect a dime from shady big-shot businessmen like Jay Cooke, a personal friend of President Grant. Cooke owed the bank half a million dollars. Its affairs were in such bad shape that Douglass forced the bank to close so depositors could get some of their money back. To his friend Gerrit Smith, he wrote:

"Despite my efforts to uphold the Freedmen's bank it has fallen. It has been the black man's cow but the white man's milk."

The failures of the *New Era* and the Freedmen's bank had cost him $17,000. His never-ending popularity on the lecture platform, however, kept him very prosperous. When his agent asked him to stop talking about the Negro and his problems, Douglass picked such topics as "The Drum and Trumpet in Ancient Times." There were never any empty seats. And he always came around to what was really on his mind—the Negro and his problems.

He also continued to speak at important national gatherings. At the unveiling of the Freedmen's Monument to Abraham Lincoln in Washington in 1876, he said much that stirred his listeners deeply. Yet, somehow, he did not mention the fact that the freedom which Lincoln gave to the Negro was being systematically destroyed—in the South by violence; in the North by a government which tried not to notice what was happening.

He was silent, too, about the political deal that broke the Presidential election tie of 1876. Both candidates wanted to please the nation's businessmen who cared less about civil rights in the South than they did about timber, mining and railroad rights. There were fortunes down south just waiting to be made. And the freedmen, "put back in their place," would tote that barge and lift that bale at very reasonable rates, or else. The deal was this: the Democratic contender, Samuel J. Tilden, conceded the election. The Republican, Rutherford B. Hayes, became President and pulled the last remaining Federal troops out of the South. After twelve years of Reconstruction, the former rebel states could run things to suit themselves again.

Douglass felt that watchful silence was the best policy for that moment. The lily-white Democratic party was dedicated to the suppression of Negro rights. The Republican party, though no longer good enough, seemed the lesser evil, most Negroes bitterly agreed. To soothe them, President Hayes named Frederick Douglass as U. S. Marshal for the District of Columbia.

The new marshal soon spoke out again. Two months after his appointment, he attacked Jim Crow conditions in Washington as "most disgraceful and scandalous." There was an outcry and a petition from the capital's leading businessmen: "Dismiss him!" Hayes didn't dare. Later that year, before another audience, Douglass criticized the President as the man who "withdrew our few troops from the South" and "recognized the shot-gun governments of South Carolina and Louisiana." No one ever succeeded in putting a muzzle on Douglass.

He was a healthy, vigorous sixty-four when President James A. Garfield appointed him Recorder of Deeds for the District of Columbia and he was another year older when his wife Anna Douglass died in 1882. "Mother was the post in the center of my house and held us to-gether," he wrote. Still, he had always regretted that she could not bring herself to be more than a shy, hard-working homebody during their forty-four years to-gether.

Eighteen months later he married forty-six-year-old Helen Pitts, his white, college-educated secretary in the Recorder's office. Neither of their families was pleased. Segregationists were furious. Many Negroes felt Douglass was guilty of disloyalty to Negro womanhood. Smiling, Douglass explained his marriage just proved he was not biased: "My first wife was my mother's color; the second, the color of my father." It was a good marriage.

President Grover Cleveland, a Democrat, kept Doug-lass in office for ten months after the former administra-tion had ended. Then Douglass resigned and sailed with his wife for a year-long European tour. This time he set foot in England not as a refugee but as a distin-guished American—a maker and shaper of his country's history.

President Benjamin Harrison, a Republican, in 1889,

appointed Douglass U. S. Minister to Haiti, the independent Negro republic in the Caribbean. Douglass resigned two years later, however, because he disagreed with his government's treatment of Haiti.

At home one July day in 1890, Douglass received a visit from Mary Church Terrell, a young school teacher.

"I've just had news that Tom Moss, a friend of mine, was killed," she said.

"Killed?"

"Lynched, Mr. Douglass." Her lips twisted with grief and anger. "Lynched!"

The old man bowed his head. He knew the meaning of the word: torture, hanging, burning at the stake, the mutilation of a lifeless body. Negroes could be lynched for anything in the South—for insulting a white person, for turning down a poorly paying job, for being unpopular, for complaining about being cheated. Tom Moss was only one of eighty-five Negroes lynched that year. The old man and the young woman went to see President Harrison who listened, said little and did less. But Douglass stood fast on "the watch tower of human freedom." He raised his still powerful voice in public protest not only against the crimes of the lynch mobs but against the "who cares?" attitude of the whole country:

"The men who break open jails and with bloody hands destroy human life are not alone responsible. They simply obey the public sentiment of the South—the sentiment created by wealth and respectability, by the press and the pulpit. Let the press and the pulpit unite their

power against the cruelty, disgrace and shame that is
settling like a mantle of fire upon these lynch law states,
and lynch law itself will soon cease to exist. Nor is the
South alone responsible. The sin against the Negro is
both sectional and national; and until the voice of the
North is heard in emphatic condemnation and wither-
ing reproach, it will remain equally involved with the
South in this common crime."

At seventy-eight, Frederick Douglass knew that time
must be running out on him. He had a yearning, and he
had a right, to walk among the trees of Cedar Hill where
he and his wife, and often his grandchildren, lived in
a twenty-room house. He liked to step out on his bal-
cony, look down toward the Anacostia River and across
to the Capitol dome. When he did, he knew that the
comfortable idleness of old age was not for him. There,
under that dome, was the power from which his people
were still being fenced off. Under that dome the future
of his people was being written and rewritten every day.
He was tired, but he was not about to lay his burden
down.

At the beginning of 1895, he was still traveling. In
Providence, Rhode Island, a youth came to him and
asked:

"Mr. Douglass, you have lived both in the old times
and in the new. What have you to say to a young Negro
just starting out? What should he do?" The old lion
raised his head and said: "Agitate! Agitate! Agitate!"

On February 20, Douglass attended a meeting of the
National Council of Women. He came home to have

dinner and to go, afterward, to his lecture engagement at a nearby church. Meanwhile he and Helen talked about the kind of day it had been. When he dropped suddenly to his knees, she thought he was dramatizing something that had happened at the afternoon meeting. But as she watched him sink down, down, to his full length on the floor, she understood he was not play-acting. Breathless with fear she knelt at his side. He was dead.

The telegraph keys chattered and the printing presses clanked the solemn news across the country. The cables carried it silently underseas. And the world responded with sorrowing remembrance of the man and his greatness.

"From first to last, his was a noble life," said an editorial tribute in the *London Daily News*. "His own people have lost a father and a friend. All good men have lost a comrade in the fight for the legal emancipation of one race and the spiritual emancipation of all."

In Americus, Georgia, Negro citizens met to mourn and to contribute "out of our poverty and still-existing oppression" to a fund for a memorial. In the minutes of their meeting they wrote: "No people who can produce a Douglass need despair."

But who would there be now to stand upon the watch tower?

ROBERT SMALLS

CHAPTER III

CHARLESTON PILOT
⊱ Robert Smalls ⊰

Everybody was at the Craven Street jail to see a thief hanged. Except Lydia Smalls. On that fifth April morning of 1839, she had more urgent business, the birth of her male child, Robert.

Lying in her cabin behind Henry McKee's fine house on Prince Street, Lydia looked at her whimpering infant and dared to have hopes for him. She could hardly name them—hope that he would win his master's favor, that he would not have to be a field hand; hope, underneath and above all others, that he could one day, somehow have his freedom.

Beaufort* on Port Royal Island, was not the worst place in South Carolina for a slave child to be born. It was *the* big town in the clutter of Sea Islands that lie along the Atlantic coast between Charleston and Savannah, like a carelessly dropped jigsaw puzzle. Port Royal, Lady's, St. Helena, Edisto, and a dozen others— these were plantation islands, long held in families who counted their slaves and their cotton bales by the hundreds and their acres by the thousand.

* Pronounced "Bew-fert"

Out on the plantations, a slave's life was hard. In Beaufort it was easier. Living within sight of each other the planters felt some need to live up to their position as gentlemen. A gentleman's servants must not look shabby or mistreated. A gentleman sometimes showed kindness or generosity to those beneath him. This and nothing more was the trickling fountain of Lydia's hopefulness. Even in Beaufort, however, slave children were neither ornaments nor pets. One early morning Lydia collared little Robert as he pushed open the cabin door.

"Hold on there, young 'un. You ain't goin' nowhere."

As the child looked at her wonderingly, she told him what his future held in store:

"Master Henry say it's time you started earning your keep. You're goin' on six now, old enough, he say, to be some use around the place." She looked away and continued in a softer tone, "He done tol' me, and I'm tellin' you. Now get on over to the house, my baby, and get yourself started."

Starting was easier than stopping. He ran errands, carried out slops, blacked boots, polished doorknobs, swept the front walk. In the barn, he cleaned stalls, oiled harness, washed muddy carriage wheels.

Little Robert liked Beaufort. There were shrimp to catch and crabs to net. There was water in which to swim and learn the handling of small boats. Often there was good eating.

Henry McKee was pleased with him. "He's a likely little hand," he said to his wife.

Little Robert found Beaufort to his liking. There were shrimp to catch at the river's edge, crabs to net along the Bay Street sea wall.

"Much *more* than likely," Mrs. McKee replied. "I expect he'll bear some watching as he grows."

But Robert, watching his master, learned the behavior of the Low Country whites. From the plantation slaves on Lady's Island, he learned the strange Afro-English called Gullah. He also learned to respect the strength of soul, the secret wisdom and the dignity of his Gullah kinfolk.

When Robert was twelve, McKee sent for him. "Can't keep you round here any longer, boy," he said. "I'm moving to a smaller house."

Anxiety widened Robert's eyes. "M-M-master? What you gon' do with me?"

"Easy, boy. I'm not about to sell you. I'm taking you to Charleston to hire you out. Mrs. Ancrum, your mistress Jane's sister, has room for you in her yard."

Charleston in 1851 was a place of wonders to behold. Handsome houses, soaring church spires, bewildering shop windows; burly steamboats and graceful sailing ships in the wide harbor, and people everywhere.

Robert was rented to a city contractor as a street-lamp lighter for four dollars a month. A few months later he was waiting on table at the Planters Hotel. He earned more for McKee that way, and a little for himself, but it was dull work. He obtained Master McKee's permission to change jobs. For a year and a half he ran a horse-operated hoisting rig on the docks. At fifteen, not yet grown to his full five-feet-five, he bossed a crew of stevedores.

John Simmons, Robert's employer, was also a sail-

By the time he was fifteen, he was a foreman in charge of a crew of stevedores.

maker and ship rigger. Short-handed, Simmons taught him the skills of fitting out boats. To change the slant of a mast or the cut of a sail, Robert was sent on test cruises among the Sea Islands. Alone in a small boat, he practiced the art of getting safely past hidden rocks, of navigating narrow channels, of easing through shoals against an outgoing tide.

"He's got the makings of a right good pilot," Simmons boasted. Hannah Jones, one of Samuel Kingman's servants, thought he also had the makings of a good husband. Robert was pleased with what she thought.

Permission to get married was no problem but they could have a home together only if their masters would also allow them to hire their own time. McKee agreed to accept fifteen dollars a month. Kingman settled for seven. The married life of Robert, seventeen, and Hannah, a littler older, began on December 24, 1856, in comparative luxury—two rooms above a stable, four wobbly chairs, a table, and a few chipped dishes.

They were happy, but marriage vows made in slavery were small comfort to slaves. Their baby, Elizabeth Lydia, born February 12, 1858, was not theirs. Neither was little Robert, born three years later. They belonged by law to Samuel Kingman. It did no good for Robert to tell himself that McKee and Kingman were kind masters. His pulse beat with the steady discontent of slavery that Frederick Douglass explained so simply:

"Give a slave a bad master and he aspires to a good master; give him a good master and he wishes to become his own master."

That was what Robert Smalls wished. Ships from the North, travelers from the West brought him news that fed his wish. There was war in Kansas to decide whether the territory should be slave or free. There were fierce attacks on slavery in Congress. Abraham Lincoln, candidate for the Senate in Illinois, believed that "This government cannot endure permanently half-slave and half-free."

Meanwhile there was only one thing he, himself, could do—earn the eight-hundred-dollar price Kingman had set on Hannah and little Elizabeth. Days, Robert Smalls sailed on Mr. Simmons' business. Nights, pointer in hand, he studied charts and maps, determined to become the best pilot afloat. By the time Lincoln was elected President in 1860, Robert and Hannah had saved seven hundred dollars.

Then South Carolina broke away from the United States. Most of the other slave states also seceded* and the Confederacy was formed. New Southern regiments took over the Federal buildings and the waterfront forts. Only Fort Sumter, in the middle of Charleston Harbor, was still held by U. S. Army troops. During the winter months of 1861 it sat surrounded by the big shore guns, cut off from help by sea or land. In April the guns roared. Sumter surrendered. The war was happening. It was too late to think now of buying freedom. The future was a giant question mark.

For people of Robert's color it started out to be a strange war. It was really about *them*, the four million

* Except Missouri, Kentucky, Maryland, and Delaware.

Alone in a small boat, he practiced the art of navigating.

enslaved, yet they were not a part of it. Smalls still had to earn money for Henry McKee. In July 1861, he hired out for sixteen dollars a month as a deck hand on the *Planter,* which her owner, Captain John Ferguson, was renting to the Confederate government. She was a steamboat, 147 feet long, 50 feet wide. Built for shallow water, she could carry 1400 bales of cotton or 1000 fighting men. And she was especially valuable because she could ride through shallow water.

Smalls was made wheelsman, closest a slave could get to the title of "pilot." All summer the *Planter* hauled workmen, materials, soldiers and guns to fortify the Sea Islands. Early that November a Northern fleet entered Port Royal Sound and knocked out the new forts. The scenes of Robert's childhood, including Beaufort, fell under Union rule. With Hilton Head as a base, the Union Navy set up a blockade of Charleston Harbor.

The planters ran off. McKee and his family fled to Mrs. Ancrum in Charleston. But the rich earth and Smalls' strange-talking, hard-working cousins on Lady's Island remained. They would work, and the cotton would grow, if the Yankees gave them half a chance. Every wind that blew from Port Royal carried the scent of freedom, and Robert Smalls took deeper breaths from day to day. He had to talk to Hannah.

"There must be some way to get to Port Royal."

"Roads full of patrollers," Hannah replied. "Woods full of soldiers and rivers full of picket boats. You're talking foolishness, man."

"I'm thinking of sailing to Port Royal in the *Planter*."

Hannah shook her head disbelievingly. "How you gonna get me and the children on board? And what about when we get near Sumter and they blow us clean out of the water and straight to our Maker?"

"It don't have to go that way," Robert argued. "It's only seven miles to the blockade boats. I'll think of something."

The "something" turned out to be a broad-brimmed straw hat belonging to the *Planter*'s Confederate commander. Alfred Gridiron, the fireman-engineer, clapped it on Small's head for a joke one afternoon when the three white officers went ashore for the night. The Negro crewmen laughed.

"Look at Bob. Doggone if he ain't a ringer for ol' Cap'n Relyea. Same build, same gait. Just a little darker, is all." Smalls laughed the hardest because he suddenly saw a joke big enough to last them their lifetimes, if they lived through the making of it. He explained it to them and in the first hours of May 13, 1862, they were ready.

The *Planter* lay at Southern Wharf, her boilers cold in the engine room, her officers warm in their beds at home. Fifty yards inshore, the sentry at General Ripley's headquarters sang out "One o'clock and all is well." Robert smiled in grim agreement as he and Alfred stepped out of the captain's cabin carrying a load of pistols and rifles. They distributed the weapons to the other six men. Then they waited.

Robert spoke to Hannah about running away in the Planter.

At three in the morning Smalls said to Alfred, "Get up steam." At three-thirty, he took the wheel. The *Planter* chugged upstream and anchored near Atlantic Wharf. Aboard the steamer *Etowah*, Negro seamen had kept five womenfolk and three children of the *Planter*'s crew in hiding since nightfall. Hannah, Elizabeth and little Robert were among them. All were transferred to the *Planter* by rowboat. Then the steamer headed into the open waters of the bay. Approaching the danger point, Smalls turned the wheel over to Sam Chisholm. Then he slipped into Relyea's gold-braided coat, pulled the floppy straw hat down on his head and leaned on the windowsill of the pilothouse with arms folded. A few minutes later, holding his pose, he was staring into the muzzles of Sumter's deadly artillery.

Now!

Lazily, Smalls reached up for the cord of the steam whistle and signaled—three long, one short. An endless moment later, the order: "Pa-a-a-a-ss the *Pla-a-an-tu-u--uh!*" So far, so good. Beyond the range of the harbor guns, Smalls signaled the engine room for full speed ahead, straight for the Union fleet. The lookouts on Sumter saw, and gave the alarm, too late.

Jebel Turner hauled down the Confederate ensign and raised the white flag of truce, a bedsheet, while Smalls steered for the USS *Onward*. Aboard the blockader drums called the crew to their battle stations. A row of cannon pointed at the stolen steamer. At last, Lieutenant Nickels, aboard the *Onward*, shouted, "What vessel are you? And state your business!"

"The *Planter* out of Charleston," Smalls megaphoned, "come to join the Union fleet." When he found his voice, the lieutenant called back, "Keep away from your guns and stand by to be boarded!"

Under Navy guard, the *Planter* steamed to Hilton Head later that day. Admiral Samuel F. Du Pont, commander of the Union fleet, interviewed the runaway pilot and learned there was icing on the cake Smalls had brought—six Confederate cannon plus valuable military information. The mouth of the Stono River, Charleston's "side door," was undefended, Smalls reported.

"The *Planter*, its crew, and the women and children will go to Beaufort," said Du Pont. "You'll stay here. I'm sending a squadron tomorrow to scout the Stono River. You'll be pilot aboard the command vessel."

Robert Smalls, twenty-three years old, felt a foot taller. He was never going to need Captain Relyea's hat again.

"Mas—uh—Mr. Du Pont, what about . . ." The Admiral interrupted.

"Yes. I will inquire. If the *Planter* is judged a captured prize of war, you and your men will come into a handsome amount of money."

Reporting to Secretary of the Navy Gideon Welles, Du Pont wrote:

". . . The bringing out of this steamer would have done credit to anyone . . . This man, Robert Smalls, is superior to any who has yet come into the lines, intelligent as many of them have been. His information has been most interesting, and of the utmost importance.

I do not know whether the vessel will be considered a prize; but, if so, I respectfully submit the claims of this man Robert and his associates."

In a week's time, Smalls was the North's outstanding naval hero. Newspapers and magazines printed every fact they could get.

For eight weeks Smalls took the *Planter* down the North Edisto and up the Stono carrying men and materials for a big push against Charleston. Then a Northern general blundered; the expedition was defeated. The *Planter* was an armored U. S. Navy gunboat now, under command of a Lieutenant Rhind, but its pilot was without title, rank or pay. He wasn't even legally free. All "displaced" slaves were still classed as "contraband," the military word for captured enemy property. Many were enlisting in the Navy though they got neither equal pay nor equal ratings with their white shipmates. Smalls continued as a civilian pilot. As for the prize money, the Navy decided the *Planter* was worth $9168 and Congress voted to pay half that amount. As leader of the party, Smalls was awarded $1500 but he was more hurt than pleased. The boat and her cargo were easily worth $75,000. *That* was the amount he and his men should have gotten half of. Well, that would have to wait. Major General David Hunter, supreme Union commander of the Department of the South, wanted to see him.

In early May, 1863, the general had asked permission to enlist a Negro regiment which he was training unofficially. Now, in mid-August, he was still waiting to hear "yes" or "no."

"I'm sending you to Washington with Chaplain Mansfield French of the Army hospital here," the general told Smalls. "I expect you to bring back official word making the South Carolina 1st Volunteers a part of the Union Army." General Hunter could have sent someone else but he wanted President Lincoln and Secretary of War Edwin M. Stanton to meet Robert Smalls, a living answer to those who still doubted that slaves would fight for their freedom. The chaplain and the pilot returned from Washington with an order permitting General Rufus Saxton, military governor of the area, to form Negro army units.

Robert went north again almost immediately. At public meetings he spoke of the thousands of contrabands taking refuge under Union rule, and of the help they needed to start a new life. In New York, a large audience cheered wildly as he received a specially designed medal showing the *Planter* leaving Charleston.

Returning to Beaufort, he found his vessel transferred from the Navy to the Army. He took her on a raid up South Carolina's Broad River, leading a string of gunboats. Soldiers from the *Planter* went ashore, attacked a troop train and were driven back. The *Planter* pushed her gangplank out and withstood heavy fire for several hours to save her troops.

Beaufort was his home now but Charleston still claimed him, and wanted to hang him. Five Charleston men, four of them white, eased into Beaufort one night, looking for him. Seized by soldiers, they admitted they were trying to earn a $4,000 reward by kidnapping him.

Facing them, Smalls said, "I'll be back in Charleston, bringing the United States Navy with me." He soon had a chance to try it, too.

In April 1863, Admiral Du Pont ordered nine iron-clads, a new type of warship covered with metal plates, to attack Fort Sumter. Smalls was especially assigned to the *Keokuk*, as Lieutenant Rhind's pilot. Close up, the *Keokuk*'s guns blasted away at the massive walls of Fort Sumter. An enemy shell took the wheelsman's head off as Smalls stood beside him. Blinded by blood and smoke, the pilot grabbed the back-spinning helm and held the *Keokuk* in firing position until he heard the signal to retire.

Returning to his regular duties, Smalls was at the *Planter*'s wheel on a run down Folly Island Creek when rebel batteries opened fire. The danger was real and Captain Nickerson, the vessel's new commander, couldn't face it. Bursting into the pilothouse, he yelled, "Beach the boat, Rob, before they kill us all. We'll surrender!" Surrender meant almost certain death for every Negro aboard. Smalls brushed Nickerson aside and shouted to his crew, "Man the guns! Fire at will! And keep on firing!"

The frightened officer stumbled below to hide in the coal bunker while his Negro crew blazed away and his Negro pilot held to his course. Rebel shells hit the vessel's smokestack. One exploded against the armor of the pilothouse. Half blind from powder burns, Smalls brought the *Planter* back to her berth, wondering if he was in trouble for disobeying Captain Nickerson. He was not. Colonel Elwell, in command of the Quartermasters Department, issued an order:

"You will please place Robert Smalls in charge of the United States transport *Planter*, as captain. He is an excellent pilot, of undoubted bravery, and in every respect worthy of the position. This is due to him as a proper recognition of his heroism and services." What's more, $150 a month went with the new rank.

So much had happened since he steamed past Sumter wearing Relyea's hat. In Beaufort he had found his mother. She lived in his house now instead of the Mc-Kee's back yard. Little Robert had died, and Sarah, his "Union baby" was born. Now he had another voyage to make. War and weather had laid heavy hands on the *Planter*. He had to take her to Philadelphia for new machinery and overhauling.

The overhauling lasted six months, long enough for Smalls to get some sorely needed equipment of his own. He hired two tutors, one in the morning, another at night, who taught him reading and writing.

Newly powered and painted, the *Planter* anchored off Hilton Head on Christmas Eve, 1864. General William T. Sherman's troops were in Savannah after cutting the Confederacy in two. Tens of thousands of slaves had followed them, as other thousands had followed Union raiders to Port Royal. Before marching again Sherman issued an order to provide for these displaced and starving freedmen. They were to be given forty-acre farms on the Sea Islands and on lands reaching back thirty miles

During the overhauling of the Planter, *Robert Smalls hired two tutors and studied morning and night.*

from the coast between Charleston and the Savannah River in Florida.

Smalls transported boatloads of freedmen to their new farms under a U. S. Army contract which gave him full responsibility for the business affairs and the navigation of the *Planter.* He got almost $2000 a month to pay and feed his crew, and himself. Early in 1865 he bought Henry McKee's old house on Prince Street for $700 in a tax sale.

By February, the Union blockade at last had done its work. Fort Sumter fell, then Charleston. Colored troops stood guard amid the seaport's ruined splendor and General Saxton came to start a new administration for the city. Smalls was with him the day 10,000 freedmen gathered for a victory parade. There were marshals on horseback, Bible-toting ministers, and squads of children singing "John Brown's Body." Little wonder that Smalls, seeing Captain Ferguson and John Simmons, introduced them to the general and added, smiling, "They built the *Planter*, but I put the polish on her."

Then April 1865 came, and with it Lee's surrender. The sorrow-ridden funeral train bearing the assassinated Lincoln rolled west to Illinois. Southern soldiers, home again, took stock to see what they could salvage from defeat.

The freedmen, meanwhile, pressed ahead to get what freedom owed them. But with their first crop they harvested the bitter herbs of Federal betrayal. While Congress was not in session the new President, Andrew Johnson, was giving the land and the laws back to South Carolina's old rulers. Thousands of freedmen were being driven off their newly gotten farms. An all-white, ex-rebel legislature, hastily set up in South Carolina with President Johnson's permission, passed a Black Code which all but brought back slavery.

After reconvening, Congress did not help the freedmen keep their land. It did pass, however, a bill to strengthen the Freedmen's Bureau which had earlier been approved by Congress and President Lincoln. The Bureau helped the freedmen get medical care, education, and fairer treatment at work, and in their daily dealings with their white neighbors. Under the Reconstruction Acts of 1867, the voter registration books were opened to all male citizens "of whatever race, color or previous condition."

His government contract at an end, and the *Planter* transferred to Baltimore, Smalls was appointed a registrar of voters in the Port Royal district. The new voters sent him as delegate to the 1868 Charleston convention to draw up a new constitution, the most democratic the state ever had. The Black Code was abolished. Civil rights were protected. A resolution written by Smalls gave the state its first system of free public education. The period of Reconstruction had started.

A majority of South Carolina's population was Negro and a majority of the delegates, 76 out of 124, were black men. Many of them were unable to read or write but some of them were college educated. While most of the state's newspapers cried "disaster," others praised the delegates and their work. The pro-Southern New York *Herald* wrote: "Here in Charleston is being enacted the most incredible, hopeful and yet unbelievable experiment in all the history of mankind."

The defeated slaveowners were determined that the experiment should not succeed. They made political allies of the "poor whites" whom they despised as social inferiors by promising them advancement and stirring up their racial prejudices. The Ku Klux Klan was formed to take back by terror what the freedmen were winning by democratic action. Murder in broad daylight, midnight whippings and the burning of buildings became familiar happenings. Reconstruction was not an "experiment," but a bitter struggle.

The struggle began hopefully, with eighty-seven Negroes and sixty-nine whites in the state legislature. For seven years Smalls was elected repeatedly, first as an Assemblyman and then as a Senator. He became one of South Carolina's most important Republican leaders. The governor commissioned him as brigadier general in the state militia, commanding a regiment of 1000 troops.

In 1874, "the General," as his followers now called him, was elected to the U. S. House of Representatives from the Beaufort County district. In Edgefield County, meanwhile, the ex-rebels formed military companies of Red Shirts, a Klan-like organization, to restore "white rule" by force and violence. One of their chiefs was Ben Tillman, tough young brother of George Tillman whom Smalls had defeated in the Congressional contest.

The spring of 1876, and news that the *Planter* went down at sea, found Smalls in Washington. Mid-summer brought him more fearful tidings. The election campaign for a new governor was turning into a small civil war. Wade Hampton was running as a Democrat and Red Shirt cavalry was whooping through the countryside to force his election by mass terrorism against the Negro voters who were determined to defeat him. An army of

Robert Smalls became one of South Carolina's most important Republican leaders.

2000 invaded Hamburg, South Carolina, massacred members of a small Negro militia company, looted and burned buildings, while the colored population fled for their lives. Smalls' demands for more Federal troops in his state, though supported by many other Congressmen, were of no avail.

Returning to South Carolina, the General campaigned for the re-election of Governor Daniel Chamberlain, Hampton's Republican opponent. Twice Smalls spoke in Edgefield, the enemy stronghold. Driven out the first time, he came back, protected by a company of soldiers. The meeting went off peacefully though his guard was outnumbered by armed pro-Hampton horsemen.

Hampton was elected and Ben Tillman made no secret of how it was done: "We stuffed ballot boxes; we shot Negroes; we are not ashamed of it." Half-hidden fraud and open terror in Louisiana and Florida as well as in South Carolina had also left the outcome of that year's Presidential election in doubt. A special committee of Congress was chosen to decide whether the winner should be Democrat Samuel J. Tilden or Republican Rutherford B. Hayes. After months of quiet bargaining, the leaders of the two political parties reached a compromise. Tilden admitted defeat. Hayes, in return, moved into the White House and moved the few remaining Federal troops out of South Carolina and Louisiana. The freedmen were left to protect themselves the best they could and Reconstruction was put down.

It wasn't that easy, though, to put down Robert Smalls. Beaufort County sent him back to Congress in 1876, 1880, and in 1884 for three more full terms. It was 1886 before the Democratic machine could work up a shuffle fast enough to deal the General out of his seat in the House. On flimsy excuses that year, 25,000 Negroes were kept from voting and all the ballots from Lady's Island, St. Helena, and Beaufort were thrown out. Smalls explained his defeat humorously:

"They tell you that my vote has fallen off. No, sir. The vote is the same today, and more, but the Democrats have improved their methods of preventing votes from getting into the box."

Home again, the General was reunited with his daughters, Elizabeth and Sarah, with Elizabeth's husband, Sam Bampfield, and the grandchildren. But he had time on his hands—time to think about Hannah, dead these four years, and his mother, Lydia, whose life had ended with dignity in the house where she had been a bondswoman. He had less time after he was appointed Collector of Customs for Beaufort. The harbor was alive with vessels taking on cargoes of cotton, lumber and phosphate. He talked about ships all day but saying "she" about a ship was not the same as saying "you" to a wife of one's own. In Charleston he met Annie Wigg, a school teacher. They were married in 1890. Their son, William Robert, was born two years later.

For Robert Smalls life began anew. For the nation's Negro millions, an era of freedom-in-the-making was coming to an end. The Red Shirt power in South Carolina controlled the Democratic party. Ben Tillman twice became governor and forced the calling of a new constitutional convention at Columbia in 1895. He made no bones about its purpose: lily-white politics and "white men's government," one hundred percent and all the way.

Unlike 1868, there were only six Negroes, including Smalls, among the 160 delegates at the convention. From September to December, he heard debates about "legal" ways to cheat the Negro population out of its voting rights. Time and again he rose to challenge Tillman:

"Instead of this infamous suffrage bill, let us make a constitution that is fair, honest, just; a constitution for all the people." A white delegate answered, "We don't propose to have any fair elections."

Northern newsmen reported the "brilliant moral victories" of the Negro delegates, "The victory of black mind over white matter." Another wrote, "It is not Negro ignorance but Negro intelligence that is feared."

It was a hopeless situation. Smalls knew he was attending the trial of Sister Goose in a court where the judge and jury were all foxes. They would convict her because she was a goose so they could pick her bones.

Things were not going well at home, either. Annie was ill. In November he got a telegram: ANNIE DIED THIS MORNING. Stunned, he traveled to Beaufort, buried his wife and carried his burden of grief back to the convention hall. He fought on issue after issue and lost, as he knew he would. The new constitution was adopted by a vote of 116 to 7.

Back at his duties in the Customs House, Robert Smalls watched the Big Stockade being built around his people, in the state and in the nation. The WHITE ONLY signs went up in public places. The broken-down Jim Crow cars were hitched up right behind the locomotives. On streetcars Negroes sat behind the COLORED sign.

Even in Beaufort, the black stronghold which Tillman could never carry, Negro citizenship was being wiped out. The last Negro local office holders were ousted by 1903. Smalls, a Federal appointee, remained Collector of Customs until 1913.

In Beaufort, much as elsewhere, whites and Negroes led their lives separately, unequally. Yet they came closer to kindly feeling for each other than in most Southern towns. Across the South, there were lynchings by the score every year. Beaufort, proud of having none, could thank the General for one it didn't have. He was seventy-four years old that spring and sick with diabetes. Two Negro suspects in the killing of a white man sat in the Beaufort jail when news reached him that a mob from upstate was coming to get the prisoners. He called a quiet emergency meeting.

"We've got to stop them before they get here," he said.

"How?"

"We'll just spread the word around that if the sheriff lets that mob get by him, half of the white folks' houses here in Beaufort are going to get burned down."

Henry Garrett, the Customs House boatman, protested:

"Great God A'mighty! It ain't the Beaufort folks that's fixin' to lynch those boys."

"Yes," the General growled, "but if they know what this one might cost them, they'll get out there and turn that upcountry mob around."

The word was spread and the sheriff, wisely, didn't gamble. Armed deputies patrolled the roads to town and the lynch blot never fell on Beaufort's reputation.

There was no remedy for the General's illness. When William Robert came home from college with a new wife and a diploma, the old campaigner was bedridden. It was comforting to lie motionless in his pleasant room in the house on Prince Street and let his mind run on . . .

He had lived in a time of pain and struggle, of promise and betrayal. He and his people had touched freedom; then the turning tide of history had swept it past their fingertips. Well, he'd been a pilot, hadn't he? He knew that every tide must turn again. And when the moment came some lusty new young navigator would cry out *now!* and his people would grasp it firmly as a prize for all to share. He died believing that, February 23, 1915.

BLANCHE K. BRUCE

CHAPTER IV

MISSISSIPPI SENATOR
⊀ Blanche K. Bruce ⊱

The new Negro senator from Mississippi sat at his desk, watching and waiting. At last, the clerk's voice floated through the Chamber.

"The senators to be sworn in will present themselves at the desk in alphabetical order . . ."

In a few moments each of them would be escorted along the center aisle by the other man from his own state, to take the oath of office . . .

"Newton Booth, California; George S. Boutwell, Massachusetts; Blanche K. Bruce, Mississippi . . ."

Booth and Boutwell rose, met their escorts and went forward. Bruce, on his feet, turned toward Senator James C. Alcorn, his fellow Mississippian and Republican. Alcorn, holding a newspaper, was reading as if his life depended on it. Bruce got the message and stepped off alone, smartly, head up. Halfway along, Roscoe Conkling of New York caught up with him.

"Excuse me, Mr. Bruce, I did not until this moment see that you were without an escort. Permit me." Linking arms, they marched on. Such was the swearing-in of Blanche Kelso Bruce, the only Negro who has ever, so far, served a full six-year term in the United States Senate.

Back at his desk, the tall tan-skinned senator glanced thoughtfully down the long aisle with a glint of amusement and triumph in his lively eyes. He felt well prepared that March 5, 1875, for whatever might lie ahead. He had traveled rougher roads in his thirty-four years.

Blanche K. Bruce was born March 1, 1841, near Farmville in Prince Edward County, Virginia. He was the son of Polly, a slave owned by Pettus Perkinson. The name, Bruce, came from the man who had owned Polly and her ten children before Blanche was born. Even as Perkinson's property, they continued to be called "the Bruce hands."

When his wife died, Perkinson became restless. Between 1844 and 1850, he took his slaves from Virginia to Missouri and back, then to Mississippi and once again to Missouri. At home and in his travels, "the Bruce hands" were his main reliance. His motherless son, William, found a boon companion in Blanche, a year younger. And Polly made the little white boy feel like a member of her large family.

Blanche sat through much of his young master's schooling and William made his tutor teach Blanche too. This may have been a shrewd idea of Polly's.

Certainly the Perkinsons and "the Bruce hands" had more personal appreciation for each other than was usual between masters and slaves. On his Missouri plantation the master gave each of them an acre to grow their own tobacco for market. Thus, Blanche's older brothers each earned about $70 a year in cash to spend on a Sunday suit, sugar, white flour and coffee. In return, they gave Perkinson hard work and loyalty.

Growing to young manhood, Blanche and William Perkinson remained friends. During the Presidential campaign of 1860, William was among those slaveholders who were against secession. When the Civil War broke out, he wanted to join the Union militia in Missouri. His father's wishes forced him into the Confederate Army in 1862.

Blanche, strong, brainy, and twenty-one, decided this was a good time to break the chain that held him to slavery. He wrote, years later:

"After the firing on Fort Sumter I concluded that I would emancipate myself. So I worked my way to Kansas and became a free man before the Emancipation Proclamation was issued by President Lincoln."

In Lawrence, Kansas, he opened and taught the state's first elementary school for Negro children. At the same time, with some of his small earnings, he paid a minister to give him advanced tutoring. When Missouri passed its own emancipation law in January 1865, Bruce was back in the state, first as a schoolteacher, then as a printer's apprentice in Hannibal. He wanted to get more education. But how?

George Cornelius Smith, a Kansas friend, wrote to him from Oberlin College in far-off Ohio.

"Come," the letter said. "Negro students are accepted here." Long afterward, Smith wrote: "Bruce joined the class and was, from the start, its recognized leader. Especially this was true in mathematics."

After a year, Bruce's money ran out. He wrote letters for financial help. When his requests were turned down, he said to Smith:

"I am truly glad the money did not come. I shall leave for St. Louis tomorrow. I can and will win my way without it. There is a place for me, and money too. Both shall be mine."

For the next two years, the self-made freedman wandered. He worked on the steamer *Columbia* running between St. Louis, Missouri, and Council Bluffs, Iowa, then tried his luck in Arkansas and Tennessee. In Memphis, he met a man who invited him to hear a speech by James Lusk Alcorn, a former Mississippi slaveholder and Republican candidate for governor. Bruce went, listened, met Alcorn, and decided that Mississippi was *the place*. And a remarkable place it was in those years.

Negroes made up more than half of Mississippi's 800,000 population. When their right to vote was guaranteed by the Reconstruction Acts of 1867, they began to exercise political power. Seventeen freedmen and 49 whites, all Republican, controlled the 1868 convention of one hundred delegates who met in Jackson to write a new state constitution.

The freedmen knew that emancipation without a share in the power of government would be an empty blessing indeed. But they had ballots in their hands. They would use them to get their dreamed-of opportunities for education, a better living, justice, human treatment from masters who had owned them and poor whites who had scorned them. From their ranks hundreds of ex-slaves were rising to become able organizers and spokesmen for Negro citizenship.

This was the Mississippi to which Blanche K. Bruce came in February 1869. Soon after his arrival he was made Conductor of Elections in Tallahatchie County. That year 90,000 Negroes and 15,000 whites throughout the state registered as Republicans. In the fall they sent 110 candidates, including 35 Negroes to the state legislature, leaving only 30 seats for the Democrats. And they made James Alcorn governor by a majority of 40,000 votes.

Bruce's feeling for the state was strengthened by Alcorn's inaugural declaration in January 1870:

"The most profound anxiety with which I enter my office . . . is that of making the colored man the equal before the law of any other man, the equal not in dead letter, but in living fact."

Bruce didn't go to Jackson just to hear the governor talk. He was able to have himself elected Sergeant-at-Arms of the new state senate. For the next six years, he rose like a rocket, fueled by his abilities and ambitions, and launched by the freedmen's need for leadership.

At summer's end in 1871 Bruce was elected sheriff and tax assessor in Bolivar County. Floreyville, Mississippi, became his home. His Democratic white opponent appealed to his listeners in a public debate by saying:

"Bruce is a decent man for his color, but he was a

slave who did nothing but wait on his master. I'm here to tell you that a house servant ain't fit to be sheriff of this here county."

"True," Bruce replied. "But I freed myself, educated myself, and raised myself up in the world. If my opponent had started out where *I* did, he would still *be there!*"

That same year he was also chosen as Bolivar County Superintendent of Education and as a member of the Floreyville Board of Aldermen. He started seven new schools in less than twelve months, but being sheriff was the most important job politically and financially. Bruce did well enough to buy six lots for $500 and build himself a house. Two years later he also paid $950 for a 640-acre plantation which its owner had lost during the war.

Heading home from Philadelphia after the Republican National Convention in 1872, Bruce and James Hill, another delegate, stopped in Washington to see the Capitol. Hill, a Negro, had become one of Mississippi's most powerful politicians. In the Senate Chamber, he pointed to the imposing line-up of desks.

"How would you like to sit there?" he asked Bruce.

"What for?"

"To be a United States Senator, that's what for."

"Fat chance." Bruce smiled.

"There's every chance," Hill replied. "Don't forget, Revels* was there before you. I can put you behind

---

*Hiram Rhodes Revels, first Negro in the U. S. Senate, represented Mississippi for a little more than a year, beginning February 25, 1870. Bruce was the first and only Negro senator to serve the full six-year term.

one of those desks, and I will. Nobody can stop us."

Mississippi's Republican Party was running a fairly good state government those years. The first free public school system was established. A start was made on repairing public buildings and improving institutions for the mentally ill and the physically handicapped. The levees, those endless miles of built-up earth which kept the Mississippi River from overflowing, were strengthened. It was a surprisingly honest government, too, at a time when crooked politicians were riding high in many state and big-city governments, North and South. Mississippi had no money in its treasury. It owed more than a million dollars when it was readmitted to the Union in 1870. Six years later, it had a million dollars in its treasury. The state debt was cut down to half a million. All of this was happening with Negroes voting and holding high public offices.

Nevertheless, most whites feared they would be oppressed by "Negro rule." They had grown up believing that Negroes were not entirely human; that they had to be controlled by white people and kept busy, like troublesome children. The very idea of Negroes being able to *choose* their employers and their occupations, of going to *school,* to say nothing of helping to *run* the state, was deeply shocking to them.

There were many, though, like Governor Alcorn, who felt the former slaves deserved a chance to catch up with the rest of the country. But even they were uneasy. What was this fear that white Democrats felt, and white Republicans could not overcome for very long?

Landowners were afraid Negroes would not be as obedient and therefore would not work as cheaply as they had under slavery. Poor whites were afraid of Negro competition for jobs. It was simpler to stick to the old idea that the freedmen could never make it and that they should be stopped if they kept trying.

Stopping them began as soon as the war ended, with threats, beatings and killings to discourage the former slaves from making a new place for themselves. In spite of the Reconstruction Acts, this violence became a carefully organized crusade led by the Ku Klux Klan. The newspapers called openly for more bloodshed to restore "white government."

By 1873 this ferocity shook even such staunch Republicans as Alcorn. Having gone from the governor's mansion to a U. S. Senate seat, he forgot his brave words of 1870. He took a stand against "too much" political leadership and office-holding by Negroes. Blanche Bruce, James Hill and the other Negro leaders, naturally, broke with him. Forming his own group, Alcorn ran for governor again with Democratic support. He was defeated by Adelbert Ames, Northern ex-general who had done much to help the freedmen. The ballots Negro voters cast, often at the risk of their lives, also sent 64 Negroes to the legislature. And the legislature sent Blanche Bruce to the U. S. Senate, to sit alongside the resentful, newspaper-reading Alcorn.

Blanche Bruce was respected in the Senate for his personality and ability. His first two speeches were made to defend the freedmen's rights. On March 3, 1876, he urged the Senate to seat P. B. S. Pinchback, Negro Republican from Louisiana whose election was being challenged. Pinchback lost his fight, however.

Four weeks later, Senator Oliver P. Morton of Indiana offered a resolution to investigate the head-whipping, killing and vote-stealing by which the Democrats took over Mississippi in the election of 1875. Bruce made a long and able speech supporting Morton's resolution. He reminded the Senate that the Democrats, who had lost by 20,000 votes in 1873, were the winners by 30,-000 votes in 1875. How did they swing 50,000 voters, almost all Negroes, away from the Republican party in two years? There was only one explanation—fraud and violence.

"This is not the mad turbulence of ignorant masses," said Bruce. "This is an attack by an aggressive, intelligent, white political organization upon inoffensive, law-abiding fellow citizens; a violent method of political supremacy that seeks, not to protect the rights of the attackers, but to destroy the rights of those they attack."

With Bruce as one of its members, the investigating committee heard 162 witnesses in Mississippi. By the time the Senate reconvened in December 1876, the committee's report on "one of the darkest chapters in American history" didn't make much difference. Congress was busy settling the big Presidential election dispute between Democrat Samuel J. Tilden and Republican Rutherford B. Hayes. A few months later, Hayes, the new President, pulled the last Federal troops out of South Carolina and Louisiana and ended Reconstruction.

The Republican party, which had been his people's ally and defender, was slowly surrendering. Bruce, faced with the choice of belonging to a weak, untrustworthy party or no party at all, went along. He hoped, but doubted, that the situation would get better. During his remaining four Senate years, he watched Negro rights and opportunities dwindle away under Democratic "white supremacy" governments in the South. He became the Negro minority of one in the Senate's Republican minority party. He spoke up for his people when he thought it was wise, though he did not always speak when he might have spoken.

From four hundred Mississippi Negroes he received a petition asking the government for $100,000 so they could move to Liberia. He brought their request to the proper Senate Committee, though he disagreed with their purpose. He did agree, however, that the government should give western land and other help to Negroes who were leaving the South to escape the harshness of white supremacy. Hundreds were fleeing, as forlorn and famished as the Israelites in the desert, toward a new Canaan they hoped to find in Kansas. The movement, in fact, came to be known as "the exodus." Bruce enlisted the support of other Senators in urging government help for the wanderers, but a special Senate Committee accomplished nothing.

At a Senate memorial service for Oliver P. Morton in January 1878, Bruce made a shrewd but sincerely emotional address. It was laced with strong, tactful reminders that Morton's example as a defender and friend of the freedmen was no longer being followed in the Senate. It may be that he touched a raw spot in the conscience of his fellow Senators. A month later, during a debate on a bill to keep Chinese from settling in the United States, Bruce was invited to preside over the Senate while the vice-president was absent. It was a conspicuous honor. Later Bruce spoke against the bill on the grounds that he was opposed to all racial discrimination.

On Blanche K. Bruce, prosperous, youthful Mississippi planter and a man of influence in his party's national councils, life did not rest as heavily as it did on the Southern freedmen. He found time to keep company with Josephine Willson, a Cleveland schoolteacher who knew how to hold her head up in polite society. They were married June 24, 1878. Their European wedding trip lasted most of the summer. They were received with official courtesy and honest admiration by the dignitaries of half a dozen countries. When their son was born two years later, they named him Roscoe Conkling Bruce out of affection for Bruce's closest friend in the Senate.

His most important task during his last senatorial years was as chairman of the Select Committee to straighten out the affairs of the bankrupt Freedmen's Savings and Trust Company. This was a bank started by and for Negroes, under a charter from Congress. A nation-wide depression, poor management and careless loans had closed it in 1874. Depositors in thirty-two southern cities were still trying to get at least some of their money back. From May 1879 to March 1880, Bruce

Bruce of Mississippi was the first and only Negro Senator to serve the full six-year term.

attended every hearing of the committee. His work made it possible for the depositors to be paid sixty cents of every dollar they were owed. Which wasn't bad for a ruined bank in those days.

Blanche Bruce, just forty, left the Senate in March 1881 as he had entered it—respected and respectable, with a reputation for good work, good manners and good, though somewhat distant relations with white Southerners who sat on the Democratic side of the aisle.

A few weeks later, President James A. Garfield made him Register of the United States Treasury. This was a position just below Cabinet rank and the highest to which a Negro had ever been appointed. He was chief of a department with 146 employees. His signature appeared on all paper money issued by the U. S. Treasury.

Replaced by a Democrat when Grover Cleveland became president, Bruce returned to private life. As a Commissioner General of the New Orleans World's Cotton Exposition in 1884–85, he organized a Department of Colored Exhibits. It was an impressive showing of the Negroes' contributions to the nation's wealth—everything from growing cotton to the invention of industrial machinery.

In 1889 President Benjamin Harrison appointed him Recorder of Deeds for the District of Columbia, the post Frederick Douglass held a few years earlier. He served until Cleveland started his second Presidential term in 1893. The following year, Howard University conferred the honorary degree of Doctor of Laws on him. He also became a member of the university's board of trustees. When William McKinley took office as President in 1897, Bruce became Register of the Treasury for a second time.

The ex-Senator had been ill for several years but he was not a man who went around complaining about his health. The people of Washington and millions across the country were shocked by the news of his death March 17, 1898, at the age of fifty-seven. Newspapers, North and South, printed admiring tributes. They agreed that he had been a man capable of speaking for his people in Congress and in his party's councils. He knew how to use his strength in the endless political tug-of-war which we call the two-party system. Though Negro votes grew steadily fewer after Reconstruction, the Republican Party had greater need of them to hold its own against the Democrats. Having given up any real effort to advance the civil and human rights of the nation's Negro millions, it kept the loyalty of Negro voters by honoring a few men like Bruce.

Why did Bruce and the mass of Negroes accept such flimsy compliments? They didn't have much choice and they wouldn't have, for some time to come. In 1877, while Bruce was in the Senate, there were eight Negroes from Southern states in the House of Representatives. In 1901 there was only one, G. H. White of North Carolina. By 1902 there would be none.

But while things were going from bad to worse for the freedmen and their free-born generations, they could at least get an occasional rueful smile out of one thing. A Confederate ten-dollar bill with Jefferson Davis' picture on it wouldn't buy so much as a sack of fodder for a mule. But in far-off Washington there was a Negro named Blanche K. Bruce, whose signature on the paper money of the United States made it real. The money Bruce signed, as required by law, did not live after him for too many years. It was paper. It wore out or was lost. But the memory of Blanche K. Bruce and his career remained as the symbol of a time past and a time to come—a time of real citizenship for all Negro Americans.

INDEX